M000305401

THE
GOLDEN KEY

Modern Alchemy to Unlock Infinite Abundance

BRANDON BEACHUM

Tell A Vision Publishing
California, United States

© 2021 Brandon Brent Beachum

ISBN 978-1-09835-599-9

All intellectual rights reserved. This book may be distributed for free, but it may not be reproduced, redistributed or transmitted in any form or by any means, including photocopying, recording, or other electronic or mechanical methods, without the prior written permission of the publisher, except in the case of brief quotations embodied in critical reviews and certain other noncommercial uses permitted by copyright law. For permission requests, contact Tell A Vision Publishing.

Cover art by Vajra (Erik Seyster) and Dalien (Daniel Villalobos).

Visit goldenkey.gift to:

- ❖ Get your personal free book download code to share with others
- ❖ Play the abundance manifestation game
- ❖ Share your success and see the inspiring results of others
- ❖ Get your physical Golden Key necklace

Distributed by Tell A Vision Publishing and BookBaby.

Tell A Vision Publishing, 3090 Bristol St. Suite 255, Costa Mesa, California 92626, United States.

For inquiries, please visit www.tellavision.life or www.bookbaby.com

Index

ACKNOWLEDGMENT

Special thanks to my partner in time Karen for helping to distill my infinite perspectives, as well as my two favorite heARTists Vajra and Dalien, without any of whom this book would not have quite the same luster.

DEDICATION

I would like to dedicate this book to all those who are ready to re-member.

Introduction: Nice to Meet You Again for the First Time

Welcome to *The Golden Key: Modern Alchemy to Unlock Infinite Abundance*. First off let me say, congratulations! If you are reading these words, I would say that it is because you are ready to attract more abundance, in all its many forms, into your life. Otherwise, you wouldn't be here, because expanded abundance is what this book represents energetically, and as we will explore within the following pages, we cannot attract anything into our lives that's not a vibrational match for where we are in our personal evolution. And let me be clear, although adopting the perspectives I am about to share will likely lead to an increased flow of monetary abundance in your life, that is just one reflection of our inherent abundant nature. You are quite likely to also experience increased abundance in health, abundance in relationships, abundance in time, abundance in peace, and in every other facet of your life imaginable.

As you proceed, please know I'm not asking you to take my word on anything that I share in this book; all I ask is that you read these words with a curious, open mind and heart, and then be willing to experiment a bit by applying the perspectives that I share, and let the results speak for themselves. Fair enough? I also invite you to pay close attention to how the words in this book resonate and feel to you energetically, as I believe we all have an internal compass that can help inform us as to the validity of information. In reality, I believe there is nothing I can tell you that your Higher Self or soul doesn't already know. I can only help you remember that which you have forgotten. So if you're willing to listen with an open heart and mind, and humor me for a few hours of reading, buckle up your seatbelt, because you are in for an incredible ride!

I am going to share with you the 8 keys to abundance, which includes the Golden Key, the master key that ultimately links them all together. I've personally uncovered these keys over twenty-five years of trial, error, and deep exploration. Synchronistically, I unintentionally landed on 8 keys when writing this book. When I first shared this with my brother, he brought to my attention that 8 is considered a financially fortuitous number in both traditional and modern Chinese culture because it sounds phonetically similar to the Chinese word which means "to generate wealth". Based on the title, some of you may be expecting this book to share wealth generating techniques like trading stocks, or how to manage your bank account. However, these 8 keys are not about how you can "hack the system" or "get rich quick" by doing something external to yourself, such as, "Put **X** percent of your paycheck in your savings account each month," or "Skip the Starbucks and invest that money in cryptocurrency," or "Save hundreds of dollars by switching to GEICO." Although that all may be helpful advice, it can only take you so far. These 8 essential keys are about unlocking the abundance that already resides within each of us, which those types of strategies completely overlook. As you will ultimately find, unlocking these foundational truths is the path to infinite abundance in all its many forms, because going beyond the surface to the deeper core of our being allows us to access the profound wisdom that will be crucial to create lasting success in the new world that is rapidly emerging. This text will guide you through 8 key shifts in perspective that once used to unlock your life, can't help but attract more abundance as a natural byproduct. As the great teacher and philosopher Dr. Wayne Dyer once said, "If you change the way you look at things, the things you look at change."

In addition to reading this book, I am also inviting you to play a unique abundance manifestation game, outlined in detail at goldenkey.gift and at the end of this book. This game will give you an opportunity to demonstrate to the Universe that you are ready to generate more golden experiences in your life and begin your journey toward unlocking infinite abundance. To give you a quick overview, if you opt to experiment and play the game, you will choose to make a monetary contribution based on the amount of abundance you wish to cultivate in your life, and the personal value you place on this book. And then you are going to set the intention to use your currency contribution as a symbolic marker of how much more abundance you want to flow back into your world. You will also perform simple yet powerful exercises to help you catalyze real, tangible results. As you and the other readers play this game, magical stories of synchronicity and abundance will inevitably unfold. At goldenkey.gift, you will also have the opportunity to share your results as well as see the inspiring results of others.

Also, as we will discuss in the coming pages, I firmly believe letting your monetary currency flow when it is aligned with something with positive and pure intentions, that also resonates with you personally, is one of the key ways we accelerate more financial abundance flowing back into our lives. Which is why if you opt to play, I am going to practice what I preach by sharing 50% of the proceeds with you from anyone that you share your personal free book download code with that decides to participate in our abundance manifestation game as well (further details at goldenkey.gift). The game is designed to help anchor into your conscious and subconscious minds proof that the claims made in this book are in fact real, and to powerfully demonstrate to you your own unlimited ability to call in any and all of the various forms of abundance that you set the intention to manifest. Ultimately this game is designed to be your personal proof of concept so that after playing you feel confident to continue to strengthen and flex your abundance manifestation muscles for the rest of your life. Information and concepts are great, but equally important is knowing how to apply that knowledge by taking action, which then leads to tangible results—something I have been fairly adept at doing in my own life.

Speaking of being adept at achieving results, let me give you a little background on me and my personal journey with manifesting abundance. My name is Brandon Beachum and I am a truth-seeker and philosopher. I have also been a serial entrepreneur since childhood, and in 2011, I co-founded a company that is present day ResortShare. In August of 2015, ResortShare was named the 569th fastest-growing private company in America in the annual Inc. 5000 fastest-growing companies list. That same year, I exited ResortShare and began focusing on my greatest passion, exploring conversations about consciousness and what I refer to as the "ultimate nature of reality" on *The Positive Head Podcast* (<u>positivehead. com</u>). I am grateful to say that *Positive Head* has been consistently rated in the Top-Five in the "Spirituality" category on iTunes/Apple Podcasts for several years and has amassed over fourteen million downloads as of the time I am writing this. I am also currently stewarding *Positive Head*'s evolution on the new, late-night style, consciousness-centric variety talk show, *Optimystic* (<u>optimystic.tv</u>), and *The Golden Key* is my first book.

So how did I accomplish all of these things? How did I defy the odds and lead my company to achieve what one in ten thousand entrepreneurs is able to achieve: launching a company with only a few hundred dollars in my pocket and ultimately growing it to exceed $10MM in annual revenue, without ever raising any startup capital? How did I create a top-rated podcast in a sea of other incredible podcasters with no prior broadcasting experience and virtually no marketing? How have I achieved uncanny health, which is arguably the ultimate wealth? How have I, at the age of 46 years young, enjoyed highly fulfilling relationships and managed to truly have more fun with each passing year? I firmly believe I have accomplished all of this by coming to innerstand the ultimate nature of reality—by learning the fundamental nature of the situation in which I find myself as a human being. The good news is, you too can achieve all of this (and more), as you will come to realize while reading this book. I am not any more special than you; I have just come to innerstand the essential rules of the game of life so to speak. And one of the reasons I want to share these keys with you freely is that I know that if you win, I win—that a rising tide raises all ships. I call it the good kind of selfish, which I will explain the importance of in the coming pages.

So then the question becomes, are you ready to experience the greatest and grandest version of yourself and unlock infinite abundance? If you currently are not are not living your highest potential, what is holding you back? Many people will tell you a lack of time and money are two of the main reasons they aren't living their best lives. Time is undoubtedly the greatest resource. Unfortunately, at our current stage of evolution, most humans trade a huge percentage of this priceless commodity for money, or rather symbols that represent wealth, and yet have no inherent value themselves. But at its core, money truly is just energy. Everything is energy for that matter, and that is not just a philosophical or spiritual concept. Science has proven that all matter (and non-matter for that matter) is energy. And this book is going to show you how to transmute and alchemize all the future energies you will experience, as well as past experiences that have impacted your life. According to Oxford Languages, *alchemy* is "the medieval forerunner of chemistry, based on the supposed transformation of matter." Alchemy is most notably known as an ancient arcane process for combining and magically transmuting lesser metals into gold. The 8 keys shared within these pages will provide you with 8 expanded perspectives regarding the ultimate nature of reality that will empower you to unlock infinite abundance. If you apply the insights I am about to share as your new core operating system, this will undoubtedly lead you to a place where you can truly alchemize and transmute all of the pain and hardships you have experienced into something as radiant and powerful as gold.

That being said, if you truly want to hit the game-of-life jackpot, you have to innerstand the fundamental rules and nature of the game in which you find yourself. Unfortunately, none of us were born with a user's manual, and most of us were handed well-intended yet outdated ideas from those who came before us that have often gotten questionable results. So what are the core truths underlying the human experience in which we all find ourselves immersed in here on planet Earth? What is the ultimate nature of reality? What are the keys to utilize if we wish to begin practicing modern alchemy?

The First Key: See the Oneness

"Quantum theory thus reveals a basic oneness of the Universe."
—Erwin Schrödinger, Nobel Prize-winning physicist

As we begin on this journey, some of the things we consider, imply, and explore may be difficult to believe at first. Perhaps they will feel too grandiose or impossible, but if you notice, even the word *impossible* itself breaks down to I'm-possible. And if you're reading this book, you have most likely at least heard the concept that "all is one," which is one of those grandiose concepts that can seem hard to fathom or wrap our brains around. That being said, I believe wholeheartedly that oneness is the underlying truth of existence, and an ever-growing number of people also appear to be subscribing to this same view of reality. More and more people are convinced that humanity is going through a massive evolution, and as we continue to evolve, I believe the old ways of operating from a mentality of separation will no longer lead to wealth and power the way they once did. I believe that generally speaking, within the span of recorded human history, we have been in a cycle designed so that humanity could experience the fullness of separation, the "me against the world," or caterpillar stage of our evolution, as I like to say. In this stage, history shows us that there have been countless instances where people were completely self-serving and actually achieved material abundance in the process. However, I believe humanity is now entering a new phase of evolution, the butterfly stage, where instead of being separation-centric and dominated by ideologies like "me against the world," the focus is on coming together to collaborate so that we can create a new world where there is enough abundance for every human being to not only survive, but thrive. I believe we have entered the prime time in our collective evolution for humanity to re-member, and come together to create from the powerful truth of our existence that is rooted in oneness.

THE BUTTERFLY EFFECT

I like to say that humanity is metaphorically moving into its butterfly stage as we slowly come back together into a state of beautiful cooperation and unity. Currently, as I write this book in late 2020, COVID-19 has demanded that the whole world cocoon itself and take a sacred pause for the first time in recent history, and it has inadvertently forced us to step back and take a long hard look at the state of the world and much of the injustice we have traditionally accepted, or just turned a blind eye to. We are starting to see an ever-increasing number of outdated structures and modalities that no longer serve us crumble. I believe 2020 will be looked back on as the year humankind moved into its "COVID Chrysalis." If you look closely at the journey of the breathtaking butterfly, it starts out as a funky little caterpillar that basically eats everything in its path with reckless abandon, oftentimes severely damaging plants and trees in the process. This is very similar to humankind's evolutionary journey throughout recorded history, doing unnecessary harm to Mother Earth, our fellow animals, and even purposely harming each other due to our narrow-sighted, separation-based perspectives and self-serving agendas.

However, at a crucial point in the caterpillar's evolutionary journey, when it has done all the consuming and destroying it is divinely designed to do, suddenly new cells called imaginal cells begin popping up within the caterpillar. The imaginal cells contain the template for the butterfly that will be born. At first, the caterpillar cells view these imaginal cells as foreign invaders, and quickly identify and destroy them, but over time, more and more imaginal cells begin to appear on the scene. They start working together, until eventually the tide turns within the caterpillar, and the imaginal cells are the new dominant force that takes control. At this point the caterpillar cells begin breaking down, and the caterpillar enters into its pupa stage, where it goes into a protective chrysalis so its full metamorphosis into the butterfly can begin. The caterpillar cells and all of the destruction that they precipitated now disintegrate into a goo that acts as fuel for the imaginal cells to feed on. In the end, the destruction that the caterpillar inflicted was necessary so that the imaginal cells could have the required fuel to transform into a butterfly. As opposed to the destructive regime of the caterpillar, the butterfly has an agenda that is symbiotic with nature: carrying pollen from plant to plant, helping flowers, vegetables, and fruits to produce new seeds.

Sound like the journey of any other species you know? This is a perfect metaphor for the evolution of humankind. If we view the human race as one large organism, each individual can be seen as a cell within the larger being that is Mother Earth. In the past, when the imaginal cells of the human organism would pop up speaking out about unity, unconditional love, and oneness, they would quickly be silenced, ridiculed, or in many cases even killed. However, just like in the caterpillar, the tide eventually turns. Today more and more imaginal cell-like humans are working together to begin the great shift into a new era for humanity. Of course it can look messy at this stage of humanity's evolution, just like it does for the caterpillar. But fear not, just when the caterpillar thinks its world is ending, it becomes a butterfly.

YOU'RE A STAR, BABY

If you wish to attract more abundance into your reality during this new era that is dawning on our planet, it's important to understand why operating from a perspective of oneness is the most foundational key to implement. So we are going to get a little geeky and start by looking at some of the ever-growing scientific evidence that points to this ultimate truth.

The first stellar thing to understand when you're exploring this concept of oneness is to understand humankind's origin story. We think of our bodies as beginning at conception within our mother's womb, and slowly inching closer to death with each passing day. This is a relative truth, but really, we need to expand our perspective and look back to the womb of all creation itself to get a glimpse of our true nature. The truth is you're a starbaby, baby.

When acclaimed astrophysicist Neil deGrasse Tyson was asked by a reader of TIME magazine "What is the most astounding fact you can share with us about the Universe?" He replied, "The most astounding fact, is the knowledge that the atoms that comprise life on Earth, the atoms that make up the human body, are traceable to the crucibles that cooked light elements into heavy elements in their core, under extreme temperatures and pressures. These stars, the high mass ones among them, went unstable in their later years, they collapsed and then exploded, scattering their enriched guts across the Galaxy: guts made of carbon, nitrogen, oxygen, and all the fundamental ingredients of life itself. These ingredients become part of gas clouds that condense, collapse, form the next generation of solar systems, stars with orbiting planets, and those planets now have the ingredients for life itself. So that when I look up at the night sky, and I know that, yes, we are part of this Universe, we are in this Universe, but perhaps more important than both of those facts, is that the Universe is in us... my atoms came from those stars."[10]

So from a physical perspective, the building blocks of the Universe are continually recycled. We are literally all composed of atoms that once were part of stars that lived out their entire lifecycle for billions of years in radiance, from infancy to adolescence, to adulthood, old age, and then ultimately died via a dramatic explosion—Supernova. After they finally died, their atomic remains spread out across the Universe. At some point, they reformed into planet Earth, and eventually you.

I personally find it immensely empowering knowing that the history of my physical being is rooted in the heart of a star. Whenever I doubt myself and my potential to be the person I want to be, to attract abundance into my life that seems near-impossible by most standards, I think about the profound implications of my origins and our collective potential. Our human doubts seem laughable next to the sheer improbability and complexity that all life including us humans formed from the cradle of the cosmos. When you feel small and your goals feel so far from reach, remember what you truly are. If you have ever wondered if you too could be a star, well wonder no more, you are made of stars!

IT'S ALL SPACE

The next big misconception that I would like to discuss is the supposed solidity of the physical matter that comprises the Universe. Matter is not actually the rigid, dense material that it appears to be. Atoms, which are famously known as the foundational building blocks of all physical structures throughout the known Universe, are actually about 99.999999999% space. If you removed the empty space from the atoms of all people, the entire human race could fit in the volume of a sugar cube! This puts a whole new twist on that '80s song "Pour Some Sugar on Me," eh?

And the particles that do make up this so-called matter are not actually solid at all. They are vibrating light waves of energy that are ceaselessly popping in and out of existence at an extremely rapid rate. The truth is we have no idea where they go when they disappear, or where they come from when they reappear, but we know just enough to see that they are intelligent and highly organized whenever they show up in our Universe. So as it turns out, reality works much like a film and a movie projector, because these light particles flash in and out of existence so quickly our eyes can't perceive their inconsistent attributes. These patterns of light particles flicker so rapidly that they give the illusion of looking and feeling solid, but the truth of the matter is that there really is no solid matter. And since you are made up of this ethereal matter, you are also nothing more (and nothing less) than highly organized and intelligent vibrations of light energy that the Universe is projecting onto the screen of your life. The star of your own movie.

LET'S GET SPOOKY

When you look at what quantum physics has to say about all of this, it really starts to get strange. As famed quantum physicist Niels Bohr once stated, "If quantum mechanics hasn't profoundly shocked you, you haven't understood it yet."

The phenomenon called Quantum Entanglement, or "spooky action at a distance" as described by Albert Einstein, further demonstrates the connectedness of the Universe. When you bring together two photons, they become entangled. Then, when the two photons are separated and you change the state of one of them, the other photon instantly reacts and changes also. And when I say instantly, I mean faster than the speed of light! Scientists have successfully transmitted entangled photons between a satellite and Earth at a distance of over 750 miles. Put one photon in outer space, do something to the entangled photon on planet Earth, and the one in space will instantly react. So if you have ever wondered why you can sense when something is wrong with a loved one, it's because we're closely entangled with the people that we love.

Quantum physicist Nassim Haramein also points out a very interesting signature from the architect of the cosmos that strongly implies oneness, and that the macrocosm is merely an extension of the microcosm, and vice-versa. He explains that we now realize empty space is not so empty; that the vacuum of space itself contains energy. If we look at the nucleus of an atom to observe how much of it is empty space, we find that 10^{55} grams of vacuum energy is present in a proton. Well it just so happens that 10^{55} grams is also the mass of the Universe! So essentially, there is the mass of the Universe present in the volume of a proton, which is a very, very small entity. Nassim went on to say that this confirms something fundamental to him: "It confirms that the vacuum is truly the thing that connects all things, it showed that everything is entangled, and that everything is one." [19]

So if matter isn't truly solid and everything is connected, what is going on behind the curtain of creation? Max Planck, another Nobel Prize-winning scientist and founder of quantum theory said, "All matter originates and exists only by virtue of a force. We must assume behind this force the existence of a conscious and intelligent Mind. This Mind is the matrix of all matter." [6] So what is this intelligent Mind? What is this force? Consciousness.

THE MAHARISHI EFFECT

Have you ever thought of a new idea and then all of a sudden someone invents it? At first pondering this, it might appear to be nothing more than a well-timed coincidence. But, upon further inspection there's more and more evidence that points to the reality that there's something more to this: a collective field of consciousness that connects us all.

In 1960, Maharishi Mahesh Yogi predicted that one percent of a population practicing meditation would produce measurable improvements in the quality of life for the whole population. One notable instance where this phenomenon was demonstrated and documented was over a seven-week period in Washington, DC in the summer of 1993. A group of meditators set out that summer with the intention of reducing crime in the US capital. The experiment started with eight hundred meditators and over the seven-week time period grew to four thousand participants. Before they began, the researchers publicly announced that they expected to have a twenty percent success rate in reducing crime in Washington that summer. They had the confidence to announce this prediction up-front because they had conducted this same kind of experiment previously, and had achieved a twenty percent reduction in crime at that time. Since summer is traditionally the highest crime rate season of the year in DC, this prediction seemed absurd. Not to mention, violent crimes had already been on the rise during the first half of the year leading up to the experiment. At the onset, the Chief of Police even chimed in by stating that twenty inches of snow would be the only thing that could possibly decrease crime by twenty percent in Washington, DC that coming summer. However, once the experiment started and as the meditation group grew, the drop in crime followed suit, just as was predicted, dropping proportionally with each passing week as the number of meditators increased. Ultimately, the largest reduction occurred near the end of the experiment peaking at 23.3%, when the group of meditators was at its largest. The statistical probability that these incredible results would occur by natural variation or chance is less than two in one billion. [41]

ALL IS ONE, ACT ACCORDINGLY

So now that you can see a few examples that we are made from the same stuff physically, and also that all life is composed of one interconnected field of consciousness, it's easier for you to start to See the Oneness and also begin to innerstand why it is such a foundational and fundamental key to unlocking abundance. It essentially means that at some level, all of the abundance we see in the world is an extension of ourselves — the opposite of our usual narrative that we are separate from the abundance we seek. So once we accept this, the question then becomes how do we access more of the abundance that is essentially our birthright, which up until now has been lying just out of reach. A perspective shift is key. Implement the mantra, "All is one, act accordingly," as a foundational truth in your heart and mind to begin to shift your perspective to always, in all ways, See the Oneness. This is why you'll notice I sometimes use the word innerstand, because it implies a deeper understanding, one that comes from the heart; a deep knowing, unobstructed by the human ego, arising from unconditional acceptance that all is one.

As a whole, this is going to require you to tap into your childlike wonder, curiosity, and wits to get your hands into the proverbial cookie jar high up in the pantry instead of gazing up at it salivating from far below. And for that to happen, it is going to be helpful to not only understand how to reach the container, but also to understand how to unlock and gain access to the infinite treats inside. Well, if nothing is solid and everything is simply vibrations of connected energy, could the cookie jar be just like the spoon in the famous scene from the movie *The Matrix?* In this scene Neo (also known as "The One"), is trying to bend the spoon with his mind unsuccessfully, and the young boy who is doing it effortlessly looks at him and says, "Do not try and bend the spoon, that's impossible. Instead, only try to realize the truth... there is no spoon. Then you'll see that it is not the spoon that bends, it is only yourself." So then in fact, you won't need a tall stool or ladder to reach the cookie jar. Instead, accessing it will require a shift in perspective: that there is no cookie jar, and you've actually had access to the infinite treats all along.

To summarize, our first foundational key on this journey is to see reality as an extension of Self. To no longer see it as a series of separate people, events, and resources, but rather to unlock the knowing that everything is interconnected. When you start to alchemize the old story of separation, and remember to See the Oneness, a natural impulse arises to do all you can to facilitate coming back together with the other you's/members, to help them "re-member" as well. You will also inevitably come to the realization that there is no separation between you and the abundance you desire. It has simply been lying dormant deep within the cells of your being, waiting for you to stir from your slumber.

The Second Key: Know the Illusion

"Once upon a time, I dreamt I was a butterfly, fluttering hither and thither, to all intents and purposes a butterfly. I was conscious only of my happiness as a butterfly, unaware that I was myself. Soon I awaked, and there I was, veritably myself again. Now I do not know whether I was then a man dreaming I was a butterfly, or whether I am now a butterfly, dreaming I am a man." —Zhuangzi, fourth century BC Chinese philosopher

For the Second Key, Know the Illusion, I am going to lay a bit more scientific groundwork before we ascend with the future keys into other more esoteric, non-physical, or spiritual realms, which I believe to be the source of the stream from which all abundance flows. Important to note, when I use the word *spiritual*, I am not talking about organized religion per se, as most religions typically point to some supreme power external from oneself. I am referring to your own infinite power that exists within your consciousness, outside of time and space, which as you are about to see, are illusory. Famed astrophysicist Carl Sagan alluded to the fact that science and spirituality are actually two sides of the same coin when he said, "Science is not only compatible with spirituality; it is a profound source of spirituality." [29] So what does science show us about the ultimate nature of reality? Albert Einstein was famously quoted as saying, "Reality is merely an illusion, albeit a very persistent one." According to Webster's dictionary, an *illusion* is "perception of something objectively existing in such a way as to cause misinterpretation of its actual nature." The ancient Vedic and Hindu teachings refer to our physical reality as *Maya*, an ancient Sanskrit word that translates to "illusion." *Maya* is essentially interpreted as the illusion that makes the world appear as a duality, as opposed to allowing us to perceive the truth of the Universe, that all is one. In fact, the word universe (or uni-verse), can be interpreted to mean "one song".

Could these ancient teachings be correct in implying that most of humankind has been flying blind for all of these centuries? Could this dualistic lens that humankind has been primarily perceiving reality through be the root cause that has unnecessarily led to war, starvation, poverty, and suffering for billions of people throughout history, by convincing us that we are separate from all that we perceive, and therefore lacking? Did the thirteenth century mystic poet Rumi actually have it right when he proclaimed, "You are not a drop in the ocean. You are the entire ocean in a drop"?[27] If we are indeed as vast and abundant as the entire forest and not just a single struggling sapling, perhaps health, happiness, money, and all forms of abundance, actually do grow on trees. Let's shake them a bit more and see if we can get some golden leaves to fall upon our path.

Touch Me If You Can

As we previously discussed, our bodies are 99 percent space, and to take you even further down the rabbit hole of weirdness, did you know that you never actually "touch" anything? When we are supposedly touching something, what is actually occurring is that as the atoms in our hands approach the atoms of whatever we are seeking to touch, and just prior to us making real contact, atomic forces stop us from doing so. What we are really feeling when we think we are touching something is the mutual atomic repulsion between our hand and the other object from a very small distance. So what this means is nothing ever truly touches anything!

Second Hand Information

Okay, so we never touch anything, but we can at least count on the consistency of our reliable clocks, right? Well, let me ask you this very serious question: Why should you never believe a clock? Because it's usually second-hand information! Get it? Second-hand, like the hand of a clock!? Okay, corny jokes aside, this bad dad joke actually contains some dad-level wisdom. Einstein gave us a peek into the illusory nature of time with the Twin Paradox. The Twin Paradox states that if you separated my mom and her twin brother at birth, and sent my mom into Outer Space at light speed, then brought her back a year later, she would be one-year-old. Meanwhile, her twin brother that was left behind on Earth would now be talking in complete sentences. This demonstrates to us that time is actually dynamic, as opposed to static as most of us have always believed. In actuality, time is malleable and does not always tick away in a predictable manner. [33]

THE SIMS ARE ALIVE

Now that science has proven that nothing is solid, everything is vibrations of energy, we don't ever touch anything, and time is an illusion, more and more of the brightest minds on the planet feel comfortable postulating about what actually may be the ultimate nature of reality. And a growing number have started to step forward, such as astrophysicist Neil deGrasse Tyson, to suggest that there is a high likelihood we are living in a simulation.

So what exactly is a simulation? As host Gregg Braden explains in his deep exploration of simulation theory on his show *Missing Links*, a simulation is essentially an experience that allows us to immerse ourselves in another external environment with the intent of mastering that foreign environment in a safe way, without causing risk to ourselves. [5] A virtual reality game is a good example of a simulation. It has a beginning and end, defined rules, and natural rhythms and cycles. Users have access to a reality outside of the simulation that they can tap into for guidance, if necessary. However, as technology continues to improve, it will be harder for users to tell the difference between a simulation and the real world. A day will come in the not-so-distant future when the difference between the reality at hand and a virtual simulation are indistinguishable to the human eye.

Director of the Future of Humanity Institute at The University of Oxford, Nick Bostrom, brought the topic of simulated reality to the scientific forefront in 2003 when he published the paper "Are you living in a computer simulation?" where he proposed a trilemma that he calls "simulation argument". In his paper, he doesn't directly argue that we live in a simulation; he lets us deduce that for ourselves after examining and putting to the test the only potential outcomes of a developing civilization. He argues that one of three outcomes is inevitable for any civilization:

1) A species becomes extinct before becoming post-human, which essentially means a species that has solved all the major problems that threaten their ultimate survival

2) A species becomes posthuman, but opts to only utilize low technology

3) A species becomes posthuman and continues to develop higher technology

He asserts that a posthuman civilization that continues to develop higher technology would have incredible computing power, powerful enough to run high-resolution simulations, which he referred to as "ancestor simulations". The simulated ancestors, or "Sims", within these ancestor simulations would be incapable of telling the difference from the original base reality, because the two would be essentially indistinguishable. And because any one ancestor simulation could have countless Sims within it, even if a small percentage of original ancestors from the base reality were to run these simulations, the number of Sims would be far greater than the total number of original ancestors.

Now this is where it gets really interesting. Bostrom used an algorithm to determine which of the three scenarios is most probable, and he found the third to be the most likely. As eccentric entrepreneur and futurist Elon Musk puts it, if this were indeed the case, then since there would be billions of computers or gaming consoles in a high-technology posthuman society, the odds we are in a base-level reality as opposed to a simulation are only one in billions. [4]

SO WHAT'S THE POINT?

If you consider a jet pilot in training, the point of using a simulator is for the trainee to master the necessary flying skills in a safe environment, so that they can use those skills in a future environment when the stakes are much higher. So could it be that we are currently in a simulation to develop certain skills we will need for future incarnations, or for when we get back to the "base reality" from which we originally departed when we were born on planet Earth? If it is all just a simulation, doesn't it stand to reason that knowing the rules of the game and following them is the path to lead to more abundance? When you learn the patterns and rules of a video game and diligently follow them, you achieve higher and higher scores, ultimately unlocking more goodies the more you play. I firmly believe that is the situation in which we find ourselves and the reason most people aren't as abundant as they would like to be is that they are playing the game of life and they don't really know the rules. They simply haven't found the keys to unlock the next level of their lives and as a result are oftentimes running in circles on the same old level. I think the characters on the *G.I. Joe* Saturday morning cartoon I watched as a kid had it right at the end of each episode when they said, "Knowing is half the battle!" And now that you Know the Illusion, you have a key that brings you one step closer to unlocking infinite abundance.

The Third Key: Focus Your Flow

"Where attention goes, energy flows." —James Redfield

Whatever you do, don't look at the wall. When they train race car drivers, this is one of the most important things they teach them not to do when speeding around the track at 200mph. Can you guess why? Because you will hit the wall if you focus on it! World Champion race car driver Mario Andretti, who is one of only two drivers ever to have accumulated an abundance of trophies across different styles of racing by winning in Formula One, IndyCar, World Sportscar Championship, and NASCAR, understood this concept well. He has stated that his number one tip to be successful as a race car driver is, "Don't look at the wall. Your car goes where your eyes go." My father put it more simply when I was a teenager heading out on one of my first long road trips when he said, "Keep it on the road, son." It seems simple and obvious that we would pay attention to where we want to go, not where we don't. However if we examine our inner dialogue as well as our actions, it is shocking to see how often we focus on the walls we don't want to hit in our lives.

LIPTON'S BELIEVE IT OR NOT

Many in our society continue to subscribe to widely accepted but outdated cultural narratives. For example, many people's understanding regarding something as foundational and fundamental as their own genetics is actually inaccurate. Most of us were taught that we are born with certain genes based on the DNA given to us by our parents, and that these genes provide us with a rock-solid blueprint for how we look, how smart we are, and essentially what we are capable of in life. We've been led to believe that genes don't change and that they are static. For better or for worse, we are stuck with whatever we were born with. If our father had cancer, we have a good chance of getting it ourselves. If our grandparents both died of heart failure, we are a likely candidate to go the same way. On the other end of the spectrum, we often praise those we deem as having "good genes" too. There actually used to be a Repository for Germinal Choice (aka fancy sperm bank) that only accepted samples from Nobel Prize-winners, and other supposed genetic superstars. I was actually waiting for a call from the founder for many years before I finally gave up. I never could quite figure out why I didn't hear from him. Puzzling, right?

Seriously though, we essentially tell a story of "genetic fatalism" in our society; some of us lose the genetic lottery and some of us win. Many of us have subscribed to this deterministic assumption as an absolute truth, affecting both our behavior and thoughts as a result. The rapidly growing field of epigenetics, which literally means "above genetic," has disrupted our traditional understanding of genetic control. One of my favorite past guests that I've interviewed on *The Positive Head Podcast* is Dr. Bruce Lipton, a former professor and research scientist from Stanford and the University of Wisconsin School of Medicine, who has helped lead the charge in the field of epigenetics. [24] In his groundbreaking book, *The Biology of Belief*, he shares his decades-long journey researching epigenetics. In his book he defines epigenetics as "the science of how environmental signals select, modify, and regulate gene activity. This new awareness reveals that our genes are constantly being remodeled in response to life experiences. Which again emphasizes that our perceptions of life shape our biology." [23]

Well-known author and thought-leader Deepak Chopra put it like this: "In the original model, the effects of our genes were considered to be fixed and unchanging, controlling every aspect of our physical makeup, behavior, and susceptibility to disease. Not just eye color, height, and other physical characteristics were predetermined by inherited genes, but perhaps all kinds of behaviors, from criminality to belief in God... The new model, however, portrays a more fluid, dynamic genome that responds quickly, even instantly, to all that we experience, including how you think, feel, speak, and act. Every day brings new evidence that the mind-body connection reaches right down to the activities of our genes... Regardless of the nature of the genes we inherit from our parents, dynamic change at this level allows us almost unlimited influence on our fate." [35] So as you can see, it's time for the limiting human narrative of genetic fatalism to be rewritten as an empowering story of genetic volitionism.

PLANT GOOD SEEDS

Our beliefs, as well as how and where we focus our thoughts and energy is crucial. Another popular experiment that demonstrates this involves sending thoughts and intentions to two different plants over a period of time. In 2018 the furniture giant IKEA conducted this experiment very publicly for the Bully A Plant experiment in support of Anti-Bullying Day, which involved students at a school in the United Arab Emirates. During the experiment, two essentially identical plants were kept under separate controlled enclosures and received the same amount of nutrition, water, and light over a thirty-day time period. The students at the school were then encouraged to send words of praise to one plant, and send insults to the other, via recordings they made that were then transmitted to speakers rigged inside each separate enclosure. After the thirty days was up, the difference between the two plants was dramatic. The plant that received good vibes and compliments was thriving and looked extremely healthy, while its insult-riddled counterpart was very droopy and had wilted, discolored leaves. [7] If focusing our powerful thoughts and intentions on a simple plant can have such extreme effects, imagine the effect of focusing our thoughts and intentions on ourselves or on our fellow humans.

I STOPPED FIGHTING THE LAW AND I WON

Most of us have at least heard about the Law of Attraction. It essentially states that what we give energy to, whether in thought or deed, we attract into our reality. This concept has been somewhat controversial; some swear by it, and others think it's just pseudoscience. But if it is indeed a real phenomenon, it doesn't really matter, because just like any other law, such as the Law of Gravity, you don't really need to know how it works to be affected by it. If you walk off a cliff, for example, you're going to feel the repercussions of the Law of Gravity regardless of whether or not you understand gravity, or even if you aren't aware that such a thing as gravity exists. I believe The Law of Attraction, or however you refer to this phenomenon, is a fundamental rule of the game of life. And understanding this fundamental rule is a crucial step toward unlocking abundance, because like understanding gravity, understanding the Law of Attraction helps us to avoid unnecessary pitfalls. The issue is many people simply don't understand how it truly works. There is a misconception that belief is the only factor involved in The Law of Attraction, however I believe there are many factors at play when it comes to what we are attracting into our reality, and our beliefs are just one of those factors. Other factors include your past experiences and state of consciousness, the energetic offerings of society and the collective consciousness, as well as your *karma* and *dharma*. *Karma* and *dharma* are ancient Vedic terms that refer to past deeds in this and past lifetimes, and your soul's grandest expression of service in this lifetime, respectively.

So as you can see, there are a lot of factors at play when we are cooking up what we wish to experience. A lot of people think the Law of Attraction means if they sit back and imagine a delicious bisque long enough, it will just magically appear in their bowl. Anything is possible, but in addition to what was just mentioned, most of the time we will also need to take some sort of action to attract what we desire. To keep with the soup analogy, think of manifestation as a recipe, with many ingredients needed to achieve the desired result.

Every time you make a manifestation soup it will be unique because the ingredients themselves, as well as the amounts used, will always be slightly different. And even then, there are other energetic forces aside from your most immediate efforts that may lead to your soup having an unexpected flavor. So I wouldn't count on a nice bisque appearing if you're just sitting around trying to wish it up, especially since you've left out the key word in Law of Attraction: Action!

BE IT TO SEE IT

Statistics shockingly show that a significant proportion of all medical healings, including surgery, are the result of the placebo effect. Research has revealed that many people that never actually undergo surgery still display improvements if they believe that the surgery occurred![40] What this demonstrates is that belief and faith are always crucial ingredients to consider. Augustine of Hippo understood the importance of faith in the process of manifesting our desires over two thousand years ago when he said, "Faith is to believe what you do not see, the reward for this faith is to see what you believe." I like to say, "Be it to see it." Neale Donald Walsch explains it simply in the *Conversations with God* book series, which describes how most people live by the formula of Do-Have-Be. Meaning they *Do* something like work, in order to *Have* something like money, so that they might *Be* something like happy. The problem with that approach is that as the creator of your experiences, manifestation actually works in reverse. The correct formula to implement is actually Be-Do-Have. If you proactively make the decision by choosing to *Be* happy, you will find your world increasingly reflecting your happiness in the things you find yourself *Doing* and ultimately *Having*.[38] *Be it to see it.*

Your primary job is to manage your vibration and swim in the frequency of joy as you inevitably expect the path to be shown to you as to where and what you should do next. Trust and know that the answers are already on their way. It's not if, but when, and once you are shown, you will be in a state to take inspired action. When you are in alignment with your optimal path, it will always feel like it is flowing, not being forced. There will be a sense of excitement of being on the right path. However whatever action you take, it is imperative that you always do so with a healthy sense of detachment because rigid, unhealthy expectations are essentially premeditated resentments, and you ain't got time for that! Always remember if it doesn't come as you envisioned, it's okay. Because as Abraham-Hicks says, "Things always work out for me," and it's always "this or something better." [21] Sometimes you are being led to what appears to be a dead end when really that chapter of your journey just ended because you learned or got what you needed from that particular experience, and now it's time to grow in a new direction.

GROW TILL TALL

Author and teacher Derek Rydall builds on The Law of Attraction with his concept of the Law of Emergence, using an analogy of an acorn. He explains that within an acorn, the full-grown oak tree already exists in potential, but will ultimately be realized, only if the right conditions are created for it to grow. If instead of being planted in fertile soil, in the right climate with plenty of water, the acorn ends up in a child's pocket and then on a shelf in their bedroom, it will never reach its potential to become an oak tree. Derek goes on to essentially say that all of the abundance we could ever wish for our lives to yield is already inherent within each and every one of us, and it simply takes us creating the right conditions for that abundance to bloom. [28] So from his perspective, we aren't really attracting circumstances and experiences to us per se, as much as allowing the potential that is already inherent within us to emerge by creating the right conditions for it do so. Your Higher Self obviously has a very good sense of humor since you have been fishing for minnows sitting on the back of a whale your entire life!

Luckily more and more people are beginning to innerstand that at some level they are creating their reality based on what they give their energy to, but there are still many who do not. Once you start to see it for yourself, it becomes really obvious how many other people are still giving energy to that which they don't want. Whether it's the person that sits next to you at work who's always complaining, or someone ranting on a Facebook feed, many people are consistently focusing their energy in the wrong direction. We all know that one person that talks and thinks a lot about sickness and disease (or dis-ease). Have you ever noticed that these types of people tend to get sick very often and are rarely at ease? I think I was lucky enough to intuitively innerstand how important mindset is at a young age because I started telling people early in my life that "I don't believe in getting sick." As a result I've never been admitted to the hospital since the day I was born, I have no aches and pains, and I can't say never, but I very rarely get sick. Nobel Prize-winner Mother Teresa demonstrated a deep innerstanding of this concept when she said, "I was once asked why I don't participate in anti-war demonstrations. I said that I will never do that, but as soon as you have a pro-peace rally, I'll be there."

Mother Teresa understood that what you give energy to, you create more of. That's why it is so important to focus your energy on being for something and against nothing. If you don't like something in your life, the best thing you can do is give it no energy. Now this doesn't mean you shouldn't ever acknowledge something that arises that you don't prefer and just stick your head in the sand either. Identifying what you don't want is actually very helpful when deciding what it is you do want. However, it is of paramount importance that once you identify what you don't want, to then shift your energy to focus on finding a solution, rather than continue fixating on the problem. Consider that from the most expanded perspective, *there are no problems, only solutions*. Think of every thought you transmit like a boomerang. It goes out and collects like-energy to the vibration of the thought you are transmitting and then adds that vibrationally similar energy to the soup of experience you are cooking up. Another good way to conceptualize this principle is to consider a guitar string. If you have two guitars next to each other and you pluck a string on one of the guitars, the same string on the other guitar will start vibrating too, because the two strings are in resonance with each other. Well, the same thing happens with your thoughts—your string of thoughts will draw experiences to you that are a vibrational match of those thought strings you choose to pluck. So then by keeping your thoughts focused on solutions, you will attract experiences that dissolve your obstacles, rather than fortify them.

As mentioned previously, there are many factors at play when it comes to what we are attracting and stirring into our soup of experience. Even though our thoughts and beliefs aren't the only factors, they are definitely main ingredients. Arguably the most admired philosopher of all time, Jesus of Nazareth, stressed the immense power of belief when he said, "Truly I tell you, if you have faith as small as a mustard seed, you can say to this mountain, 'Move from here to there,' and it will move. Nothing will be impossible for you." Henry Ford also understood this when he said, "Whether you think you can, or you think you can't—you're right." So look on the bright side, you've never been wrong!

THE ART OF FLOW

Okay, so we know it is important to focus our energy on what we want more of, and to put no energy toward things we don't want to flow into our reality, but what do we do when we attract something we don't want or expect? The secret is to learn to surrender to the waves. I like to think of myself as a cosmic surfer that is learning to ride the waves that rise and fall, flowing with what is unfolding, not paddling against the current any longer, as that is exhausting. Anytime I catch myself feeling agitated and stuck, the moment I let go of my desire to control the situation, and remind myself to stop resisting, I instantly feel a deep sense of relief. It's as if I have burst through the water's surface, finally catching my breath. Surrendering in this way immediately eases the tension and frees up my precious energy so that it can flow toward a solution. Society has taught us to fight for what we want, to go upstream, but as Abraham-Hicks teaches, "Nothing you want is upstream!" [21] Some of the happiest people I know are those that just go with the flow of where life is taking them next. Oftentimes nomadic (or go-madic as I like to call it), they typically have no major agendas and no definitive plans. Instead they just focus on becoming more adept at riding the waves of life and synchronicity.

As you become more sensitive to reading and sifting through energies to determine where to place your powerful focus, you will also begin to realize the importance of knowing when to surrender to what is wanting to unfold that is outside of your conscious intention to manifest. Michael Singer wrote a great book called *The Surrender Experiment* that documents how his rich and fascinating life journey unfolded through repeated acts of divine surrender, allowing himself to be attached to nothing and viewing everything as helpful feedback informing him where he should navigate to next. [31] What Singer was tapping into is the art of flow, and being in the flow is a powerful place to be. Learning to flow gracefully is a skill that naturally arises as you become more aligned with who and what you truly are. The art of flow emerges as you learn to balance disciplined thought and action with surrender to every wave that arises.

When you fully innerstand how all these subtle energies and forces come together to create our experiences, you will begin to Focus Your Flow by integrating the innerstanding that you *buy* what you *pay* attention to, and it can truly start to look and feel like you are tapping into magic. The word *abracadabra* is derived from the Aramaic phrase *avra kehdabra*, which translates to "I will create as I speak." So when you use your words as your wand, indeed, you are *spelling*. However, as you chase the magical rabbit that pops out of your proverbial hat further down the abundant rabbit hole, there is another important factor to consider more than ever as humanity enters a new phase of evolution: intention.

The Fourth Key: Align Your Intentions

*"All doubt, despair and fear become insignificant
once the intention of life becomes love."* —Rumi

As I mentioned earlier, humanity is currently transitioning into a metaphorical butterfly. In the caterpillar's world, the underlying intention to take what it wants at all costs made sense during that phase of its evolution. However in this new phase of evolution on planet Earth, I believe it is becoming increasingly important that our intentions are positive and pure. Remember, compared to the destructive regime of the caterpillar, the butterfly's intentions are symbiotic with nature—constructive, not destructive. So if you want to know what the outcome of an action is going to be in the butterfly's world, look no further than the root intention. Is it love-centered or self-centered? Although selfish acts at the expense of others may have appeared to work in the past, in the love-centered world of the butterfly, those types of self-serving acts just won't fly. It is imperative moving forward that you act from a place of pure intention, considering the impact of all involved, knowing that what you put out will ultimately be reflected back.

IT ALL COMES BACK TO YOU

This realization was first driven home for me many years ago when my brother shared a lucid dream, in which he felt he was visited by my dead grandmother. At the time, my brother and I had recently moved to California from the East Coast with dreams of making it big in the music biz with our band, Kundalini. So my brother decided the best use of his airtime with our deceased grandmother was to ask her what she foresaw becoming of our band. Her response:

"You are going to get out of it exactly what you put into it."

Now Kundalini never made it big, but why? What collective energies did the five band members put into it? Did our intentions come from a pure, love-centered place? Well, our intentions weren't bad per se. One of my personal intentions when we formed Kundalini was to raise our listeners' consciousness through music, but if I'm being honest, the stronger group desire was for fame and fortune, which I'm sure you would agree is slightly less noble. Now you may be thinking sure okay, but I don't think the '80s hair metal band Def Leppard's intention to get sugar incessantly poured on them was exactly the noblest of intentions either. But there are many factors at play when it comes to what we are attracting into our reality. It's also important to consider what the members of Def Leppard were putting out energetically to garner mainstream success. Perhaps as a group they collectively had more faith they would be successful than we did, focused less on hitting the wall of failure, practiced more, etc. Besides, they may have accumulated wealth and fame, but there are many other forms of abundance as well, and who's to say their apparent success didn't come at the expense of the ultimate abundance: health and happiness. Now none of this may have actually been the case, but my point is just to share a hypothetical example to highlight that there are many factors to consider when you are examining the results of any endeavor. And remember, times are shifting; acts that elicited results in the '80s may have been less effective for my band as we were emerging on the scene in the early 2000's, as the world was further along in its transition to the butterfly stage.

THE ULTIMATE INTENTION

To add to the complexity of factors to consider, there is a natural ebb and flow of intention inherent in nature that is the underlying current of creation. We have control over our intention at a personal level, which can impact the intention at a societal level, but there is also the ultimate intention which comes from Source/God/Creator/Higher

Self/the Universe. Since we live in a freewill Universe, we can set whatever individual intention we want, but if it is not aligned with the intention of your Higher Self or the Universe, the results you get may be less than desirable. We've all heard the saying, "The road to Hell is paved with good intentions," but in this new phase of humanity's evolution I would say, "The road to Heaven is paved with aligned intentions."

One of my favorite philosophers and teachers, Dr. Wayne Dyer, wrote an entire book dedicated to this subject called *The Power of Intention*.[12] In it he explains that intention is not as much something you do as it is an energy you're a part of. He suggests it is more about connecting to the all-pervading energetic force of pure intention in the Universe that allows the act of creation to take place, or as I prefer to call it, *the Source consciousness that creates and animates all things*. Not only do you emanate from this field of pure intention, but if you align yourself to it, your desires become fulfilled and you find yourself at peace. His book was originally inspired by Carlos Castenada's perspective on intention. Castenada stated, "In the Universe, there is an un-measurable and inde-scribable force, which those who live of the Source call inten-tion... absolutely everything that exists in the entire cosmos is attached to intent by a connecting link. Sorcerers are not only concerned with understanding and explaining that con-necting link, but they are especially concerned with cleansing it of the numbing effects brought about by all of the concerns of living at ordinary levels of consciousness."[8] When he uses the word *sorcerer*, he is not referencing a wizard-type charac-ter out of a Harry Potter novel, but rather someone who lives of, and is aligned with Source. A "Source-rer" if you will. As you align with the intention of your Higher Self, the ultimate intention of all intentions, experiencing incredible things such as manifesting your wildest dreams and miraculous healings are genuine possibilities, and even probabilities. By cleansing your connection with Source, dreams that once felt impossible, become inevitable. Or as Dr. Dyer puts it, "I am realistic, I expect miracles."

So in this new world we are collectively stepping into and creating with the power of intention, it is crucial to look at the intentions we are setting and aligning with. And as you begin to innerstand that we are all extensions of one another and everything that we see, the basis of all decisions naturally becomes anchored in the truth that all is literally one. It begins to become apparent that *all deception is an act of self-deception.* A snake eating its own tail. Gandhi understood this when he said, "If you want to find yourself, lose yourself in the service of others." Why does this sage wisdom hold true? Because there are no others! Whatever I do to another, I am doing to myself, and therefore I will ultimately feel the energetic repercussions of my actions. The prayer of Saint Francis of Assisi who lived in the twelfth century is one of the most beautiful intention setting statements I have ever heard:

> Lord, make me an instrument of your peace
> Where there is hatred, let me sow love
> Where there is injury, pardon
> Where there is doubt, faith
> Where there is despair, hope
> Where there is darkness, light
> And where there is sadness, joy
> O' Divine Master, grant that I may
> Not so much seek to be consoled as to console
> To be understood, as to understand
> To be loved, as to love
> For it is in giving that we receive
> And it's in pardoning that we are pardoned
> And it's in dying that we are born to Eternal Life

I firmly believe if a person opts to adopt Saint Francis' intention as their own, it is an extremely powerful, yet simple formula for an abundant life. Instead of constantly chasing the carrot to get something more for ourselves, what if we finally stop the chase and ask the question, "How and where can I give more abundantly?" If you attract what you put out, how can you give more of what you want to experience in your life? I believe the Universe will always find a way to present us with opportunities to give to others what we want for ourselves in some way, shape, or form. This is the ironic cosmic joke that the Universe is constantly waiting for us to clue in on. When a divine opportunity to align your intentions with service presents itself, do it, do it, do it! This is how you energetically attract what you want back to yourself, because the truth of the matter is, you are always doing it to yourself. I call this the good kind of selfish, the kind where everyONE wins!

As you become more proficient at Focusing Your Flow to Align Your Intentions with the ultimate intention of Source, and alchemizing the events and circumstances in your life into opportunities to sow mutually beneficial outcomes for all involved, you will find yourself gracefully and joyfully floating in the present moment more often, and thoroughly enjoying whatever shows up. Because it is indeed true that as aspiring writer Nancy D'Souza has said, "A heart with pure intentions will never lead you astray."

The Fifth Key: Be, Be, Be

"Be here now." —Ram Dass

I have always found etymology, the study of the history and origin of words, fascinating. When you break words down, you often find their deeper meaning hidden in plain sight. I've noticed in some cases, a person's name appears to give you an indication of their character as well. For example, the former investment advisor, Bernie Madoff, burned everyone and made off with their money by orchestrating the biggest Ponzi scheme of all time. Or take the former New York Congressman, Anthony Weiner, who fell from grace after he was exposed (pun intended) for being involved in multiple sexting incidents where he sent nude pictures of himself. The Universe definitely has a sense of humor. I had to smile when I originally examined my own name, and first uncovered the message the Universe apparently wanted me to discover. In the past, I often struggled to slow down and be present in the moment. My parents have told me that when I was a kid, it was nearly impossible to hold me; I would squirm until I got away because I had much more important things to do! My full name is Brandon Brent Beachum—initials B.B.B. However, it wasn't until I was well into adulthood that I realized how important it is to just Be, Be, Be.

THE PRESENT IS THE GIFT

So in my own journey, as I continued to uncover the path to greater fulfillment and abundance, at some point it became apparent to me that the more I slowed down, was present, and could just be, the happier and more peaceful my life became. I believe there is a very good reason that two of the most popular transformational self-help books ever written are titled *Be Here Now* by Ram Dass[9] and *The Power of Now* by Eckhart Tolle.[36] They both speak to this essential key — to Be, Be, Be — that helps unlock the abundance that is inherent in the present moment. Whenever we are focused in the past or future, we are doing so at the expense of the present, and this is expensive indeed. And speaking of words holding a deeper meaning, I believe the present is called the present because it is the ultimate gift that we have been given! Too often we spend our time longing for the past, or worried about the future, which is really just a poor use of our powerful imagination when you think about it. The reality is, the future rarely comes exactly like we imagine it, and when we gaze into the past, we are often seeing through rose-colored glasses. I'm sure many of you can relate to getting nostalgic for a past relationship and only remembering the good times, but filtering out the memories of how much it annoyed you when your former partner incessantly nagged you, or kept you up all night snoring.

Some 2,500 years ago, Lau Tzu, the great Chinese philosopher and reputed author of the *Tao Te Ching*, understood the importance of living in the present moment when he said, "If you are depressed you are living in the past. If you are anxious you are living in the future. If you are at peace you are living in the present."[37] Important to note, he did not say if you are *happy*, you are living in the present. He said, if you are at *peace*. Inevitably, there will be times when you are not particularly happy, but by applying the proper perspective you can alchemize those challenging moments, by choosing to be at peace regardless of what is transpiring. The truth of the matter is, we can deal with anything that is happening in the now if we choose to be fully present. If you're ever worried about the future, I would encourage you to recall how rarely your greatest fears have actually come to pass. Your personal history is a testament to the fact that even when something challenging does emerge, you have always been able to get through it. So if you don't prefer your circumstances in a given moment, you can always find comfort in knowing that this too shall pass. As the Greek philosopher Heraclitus said, "Change is the only constant." However, on the flipside of the coin, be aware that this is true of the good things in life as well. This is another reason to be present in every moment, and appreciate the people and things we love, because change is inevitable, and the moments we hold dear will eventually pass too. The good news is, the infinitely abundant Universe can usher in unlimited new gifts on the winds of change, especially if we are vigilant about remaining in the present, so that we are sure not to miss them.

NOW AND NOT LATER

The importance of being present in the moment ultimately becomes even more clear as we begin to see that there actually is no past or future, there is only now. Both Dass and Tolle reference this truth in their books, that now truly is all that exists and therefore where all of our power lies. And as discussed earlier, Einstein's theory of relativity demonstrates time is actually dynamic, as opposed to static, and so in actuality our experience of time as linear is an illusion. One of my favorite philosophers, Alan Watts, eloquently explained how the now is all there is, and how eternity is synonymous with each and every now moment when he said, "You are this Universe. And you are creating it at every moment. Because you see it starts now. It didn't begin in the past. There was no past. If the Universe began in the past, when that happened it was now. But it is still now and the Universe is still beginning now and it's trailing off like the wake of a ship from now and as the wake of the ship fades out, so does the past. You can look back there to explain things but the explanation disappears. You will never find it there. Things are not explained by the past. They're explained by what happens now. That creates the past. And it begins here."[42] So when you begin to innerstand there is only now, then the past and the future have less of an impact on the present moment. Or as Watts also said, "The wake doesn't drive the ship, any more than the tail wags the dog!" So anytime we are overly focused on our past actions or future possibilities, we are actually giving our ability to affect true and powerful change away to an illusion. I once made a watch that just said "NOW" on the face. To this day, it is the most accurate watch I have ever seen. Your past doesn't dictate who you can be unless you decide to drag it forward with you! In actuality, we are born anew in each new now. Our powerful cause to produce effects always lies in the now, and luckily for us, there is an infinite abundance of now moments.

So as we begin to shift our focus away from a time-based perspective of reality, and the realization begins to settle in that there is no past or future and we are all floating in the eternal now, we're freed up to experience the abundance of the present moment as the gift that it truly is. Consider the time-shattering notion that a billion Earth years ago you were somewhere experiencing a different now, and in a billion Earth years, in what we call the future, you will be in another now moment somewhere else. To take it a step further, since time is actually an illusion, consider the notion that both of those past and future moments are actually happening in this eternal now moment as well. To make it a little easier to wrap your brain around, think of it like your fifth birthday party is playing out at this very moment on another channel that you just aren't tuned into. The same way you can only hear the radio station you are tuned into, even though many others are simultaneously playing on other channels.

CELEBRATE GOOD TIMES

It's time we stop the insane modern-day trend of dancing with the intention of getting to a certain spot on the dancefloor, or listening to the song of our lives with the intention of getting to the last note. Instead, I implore you to celebrate every note in the song, trusting and knowing that you will always be at the exact spot on the floor that is in your highest interest. You always have exactly what you need most in every moment, however it presents itself! Fully experiencing wherever you are in your life's journey at every moment is the ultimate goal and the path to unlocking your true potential. You, my friend, have officially arrived at the chapter of your life where it is time to stop chasing fulfillment. NOW is the timeless moment for you to Be, Be, Be and allow fulfillment to flow to you and through you! NOW is the time for you to stop playing small because you finally realize this moment is as divine as any moment ever has been or will be, and you are ready for life to take on a new golden shimmer. It is your destiny to realize that being fully present is where all the treasures of abundance await to be discovered, and being present in the now naturally leads to greater trust in the unfolding of your life!

The Sixth Key: Trust the Mystery

"The bad news is you're falling through the air, nothing to hang on to, no parachute. The good news is, there's no ground."
—Chögyam Trungpa

BEAM ME UP, WHOEVER YOU ARE

In my all-time favorite television show, *Star Trek: Discovery*, the main character, Michael Burnham, is a science-centric, highly rational, cosmic explorer who navigates through life on the assumption that everything mysterious ultimately has a scientific explanation. However, after a myriad of intense and inexplicable experiences transpire, her outlook slowly shifts, and she opens up to more mystical possibilities. She comes to terms with the truth that the more you know, the more you realize you don't know, and that that's okay. At a crucial moment in the narrative when all anchors to her known reality are rapidly disintegrating, she accepts her fate that taking a leap of faith is apparently what she is meant to do. She then turns to her crew members just before her leap into the unknown and says, "Trust the Mystery." Her words rang out to me like a bell of universal truth.

ROCK-SOLID

As mentioned in the introduction, some of you may have expected this book to at least touch upon more typical techniques to help you achieve external success through manipulation of external circumstances. But as you can see, this book is focused on sharing key shifts in perspective that fortify your foundation within so that you can build lasting success and abundance regardless of external indicators like your job title or salary. As Jesus said, "Therefore whoever hears these sayings of Mine, and does them, I will liken him to a wise man who built his house on the rock: and the rain descended, the floods came, and the winds blew and beat on that house; and it did not fall, for it was founded on the rock. But everyone who hears these sayings of Mine, and does not do them, will be like a foolish man who built his house on the sand: and the rain descended, the floods came, and the winds blew and beat on that house; and it fell. And great was its fall."

As you begin to implement the keys in this book to fortify your foundation on the rock of your reality, you will begin to attract, and train yourself to identify the unwavering abundance that appears in countless forms regardless of external circumstances. Sure, you may unexpectedly lose a job, or a partner may suddenly leave you, but you will learn to Trust the Mystery that fresh opportunities will always and inevitably present themselves. As you learn to *trust everything*, oftentimes completely unforeseen circumstances will arise that lead you to greater abundance than you ever could have found had you been on your previous path. In the new world that we are collectively stepping into, your primary job is way less about learning new stock tips, and much more about managing your vibration, learning to trust your intuition, and identifying when it is time to take inspired action and then follow the breadcrumbs of abundance that the Universe ever-increasingly leaves for you upon your infinite trail.

PARANOID BREAK DOWN

Anxiety disorders are the most common type of mental illness in the US, affecting at least forty million adults age eighteen and older every year. However, as we begin to unlock our lives with the keys in this book, we slowly move from a state of paranoia to a state of pronoia. It is believed the word pronoia originally appeared in an academic journal in 1982 in an article titled "Pronoia" published by Fred H. Goldner[15] — another great example of a person whose name suggests something about their contribution to the world. This golden word is the opposite of paranoia, and essentially means that you are highly suspicious that the Universe is conspiring on your behalf. I definitely experience pronoia, because I firmly believe that life is happening for me, not to me. And as the paranoia of disconnection begins to dissipate, and you begin innerstanding that the Universe is seeking to evolve itself through you, you can relax in the knowledge that everything is leading you to the next greatest and grandest version of yourself. Realize your only job is to follow the breadcrumbs of experience like a curious child asking the most pertinent of questions: Why is this happening for me? Once you start seeing through this lens — that *life is happening for you, not to you* — you will inevitably observe for yourself that applying this approach and perspective to the events that transpire in your life is the ultimate game-changer.

MIRROR, MIRROR ON THE WALL

To take it a step further, I believe that life is not only happening for you, but it is also happening *through you*. Your reality is simply a feedback loop reflecting you back to you, for your own good and growth. Have you ever considered that the guy agitatedly cutting you off on the freeway could actually be a mirror for your own agitation? That perhaps he is reflecting your own irritation back to you that you felt earlier that morning when you excitedly prepared your delicious Eggo waffle, only to discover someone had used the last of your maple syrup. In that moment on the freeway, unbeknownst to him, he is serving as a reflection for you. He is giving you the opportunity to see yourself, so that you may choose to consciously proact, as opposed to unconsciously react, to similar situations with others in the future. This will help you to process and release that energy that you have been putting out to the Universe as it comes back to you, and even more importantly, become more aware and intentional about the energy you are putting out to begin with.

In this way, I believe that every interaction with another

human holds a gift for us. The great Persian poet Hafiz alluded to this truth when he said, "How do I listen to others? As if everyone were my Master speaking to me his cherished last words." Who would have thought a guy giving you the middle finger out of his car window could be a cherished master? As you start to ponder the profound perspective that *your triggers are your treasures*, and that everyone around you is playing both the role of the teacher and the student simultaneously, you will come to innerstand the divine dichotomy that everything is personal from one vantage point, and not at all personal from another — *it's all just spiritual business!* Everything which transpires is just a feedback loop informing you where you are on your life's path, essentially acting as your soul's unwavering compass. Perhaps this is the syrup your waffle has been missing all along!

SWEET SYNCHRONICITY

Modern polymath Robert Grant was quite perceptive when he said, "Randomness is simply mankind's inability to perceive and comprehend God's patterned encryption."[17] What I believe Grant is alluding to here is that there is always a deeper meaning in what may otherwise appear random or merely coincidental. *Synchronicity* is a term coined by the famed psychiatrist Carl Jung, who defined it as a "meaningful coincidence." For me, receiving a synchronicity is like getting a wink from the Universe that I am on track with my highest potential timeline. Jung also said, "Synchronicity is an ever-present reality for those who have eyes to see."[22] I see it as the feedback loop reflecting all the magic that is inherent in existence back to me in a very playful and inspiring way. As we become more childlike in our playful, trusting approach to life, the Universe starts playing back! And as you begin to get into the flow of your life and learn to Trust the Mystery, that's when the synchronicities really kick into high gear. At this point in my personal journey, I experience smaller winks pretty much daily, and awe-inspiring synchronicities fairly regularly.

To give you just a few examples of how synchronicity can inspire you on your journey, I will share a few that I experienced during the creation of this book. First, the concept for the book and the unique way with which I am inviting readers to play with the key perspectives I share, came to me in a dream. I believe that when you come into greater alignment, the dreamstate becomes a way that your Higher Self/Source/the Universe communicates with you to help steer you on your path. Upon waking from this prophetic dream, I pondered what I would name my book. The name "The Golden Key" immediately came to my mind. So I did an internet search to see if anyone had already used the name for anything else, and the first thing I found was a short essay titled *The Golden Key*, published in 1931 by Emmet Fox.[13] Now I didn't know who Emmet Fox was at the time, but a bit more research revealed that he is one of the first New Thought spiritual leaders who helped to bridge the gap between religion and the spirituality-based concepts we are exploring in this book. I was amazed when I read the summary of his essay and saw that in it he shares a technique for how you can overcome any issue in your life by shifting your focus to God, which essentially elevates your vibration by aligning you with Source. He then invites people to "simply try it for yourself, and see" in a playful, gamified way, quite similar to the way in which I was guided in my dream to invite you to play a game with these 8 key perspectives — as detailed at goldenkey.gift and at the end of this book.

That was the first golden synchronicity. To me, a synchronicity as profound as this is a clear indication that I am on the right path. An even more profound synchronicity unfolded when I reached out to my good friend and incredible visionary artist, Vajra, to see if he would be open to creating the cover art for the book. Initially, I hesitated reaching out to him because I was concerned that my tight time frame for completing and publishing the book would conflict with his lengthy artistic process; however, after some consideration, I decided to reach out. When we got on the phone, I told him about my dream, my concept for the book, and the Emmet Fox synchronicity. After I was done explaining it all to him, he quickly proceeded to pull out his dream journal to read me his notes from a very elaborate dream he'd had a few months earlier, in which he was at my house searching for what in the dream was called "The Key to Everything"! The dream had been so impactful and inspiring to him that he had already started working on a drawing of The Key to Everything. After recounting his dream and describing his drawing of The Key, he said, "So to answer your question, 'Will I have enough time to create your cover art?' Well, I've already started it!" Unbeknownst to me, the Universe had magically set the wheels in motion months earlier so that my cover could be completed on time, which ultimately was made possible with some collaborative assistance from my other brilliant artist friend, Dalien.

Following that initial conversation with my friend Vajra, I remember feeling a sense of wonder and awe for the mystery of the Universe. This epic synchronicity was a potent reminder to me to Trust the Mystery! There have been many more synchronicities surrounding the creation of this book (too many to recount here), but I will share one final synchronicity story with you, if only to spark your imagination and inspire you to begin to recognize the synchronicities in your own life, that will surely continue to grow as *you* continue to grow. It occurred when I was listening to music while driving one day soon after beginning to write this book. I was thinking about the book, how I would share about it on my show *Optimystic*, and getting excited imagining the success and abundance that would flow to many people from its creation. The song "Humble in the Jungle", a MORiLLO song that samples the Kendrick Lamar lyric, "My left stroke just went viral," jumped out to me as slightly synchronistic, as I am left-handed, and I had just been daydreaming about my writing (i.e., pen-strokes) going viral. This little wink from the Universe, combined with the pleasure I naturally derive from driving and listening to music, got me into a heightened state of joyous excitement.

As I continued to play with this expansive idea, my excitement grew, and I began to fantasize about one day having a party celebrating the book's success. Perhaps I could DJ, I thought, and I would definitely play this song. Then in true childlike fashion, I dreamed of how behind the DJ booth, I would have a screen set up with visuals playing. This made me think of a clip from an Incubus music video made twenty years ago that shows two hands drawing themselves in an Escher-esque fashion. I thought how perfect this would be to have those hands drawing on the screen as a fun representation of what the lyric meant to me, with a golden key incorporated into the image as well. After about five minutes of joyfully imagining this scenario while driving in my car, I finally arrived at my destination. When I got inside, I sat down and opened Instagram on my phone. At the top of my feed was an animated drawing posted from Brandon Boyd, lead singer of Incubus, of a left hand holding an epic-looking antique key, and the animated portion of the drawing was spelling out the letters O-P-T-I-M-Y-S-T-I-C! Not to mention, I had originally gotten the idea for naming my show *Optimystic* from Brandon Boyd after I was led to it in dramatic fashion via another dream several years earlier. And now I'm getting chills in the moment as I write these words because it just occurred to me that the song for the Incubus video is called "Drive" (and this synchronicity story began while I was having a powerful experience driving). Lastly, one of the main lyrics in the song is, "Whatever tomorrow brings I'll be there with open arms and open eyes," which is essentially another way of saying, "Trust the Mystery!"

I could honestly write an entire book of incredible synchronicities that have unfolded in my life. The main point I want to drive home to all of you reading these words is that this sort of magic is in no way special to me; synchronicity is just a byproduct of what occurs energetically when you begin to use the keys in this book to unlock infinite abundance. I would go so far as to say you are hearing these words because you are on the verge of stepping into this next-level flow of synchronicity and magic in your own life! However, to do so, it is of vital importance that you begin to trust yourself more fully — Trust the Mystery — and that you don't let "fear take the wheel and steer," as another lyric in the song "Drive" states. In quite possibly my favorite quote of all time, Terence McKenna sums up this key perfectly when he said, "Nature loves courage. You make the commitment and nature will respond to that commitment by removing impossible obstacles. Dream the impossible dream and the world will not grind you under, it will lift you up. This is the trick. This is what all these teachers and philosophers who really counted, who really touched the alchemical gold, this is what they understood. This is the shamanic dance in the waterfall. This is how magic is done. By hurling yourself into the abyss and discovering it's a feather bed." [25] If you can begin to approach obstacles in this fashion you truly can alchemize the circumstances of your life into gold. Now is the time for you to Trust the Mystery and dance in the waterfall of existence.

The Seventh Key: Love What Comes

"Love is the answer (now) what was the question?!"
—*John Lennon remixed by Brandon Beachum*

FACE EVERYTHING AND RISE

When you boil life down to its essence, there are only two true emotions. Or as John Lennon puts it, "There are two basic motivating forces: fear and love. When we are afraid, we pull back from life. When we are in love, we open to all that life has to offer with passion, excitement, and acceptance." The reality is, circumstances will arise that will create fear in our hearts, making us want to withdraw from life. However, we actually have another choice: to Love What Comes, by turning toward our fears instead of away. F-E-A-R can either mean Forget Everything And Run or Face Everything And Rise, and it's up to you to decide. Award-winning poet and mystic Richard Rudd suggests the incredibly empowering notion that "fear is safe." [26] This may seem counterintuitive, but the fact of the matter is, fear is nothing more than a necessary tool that allows us to experience love. The truth is, the ultimate nature of reality is foundationally based in love, and everything that is happening, is happening for love. In essence, love is the only thing that's real and everything else is just a prop in Love's epic movie. I like to say our role as modern spiritual alchemists is to sift and shift perspectives until love emerges. Imagine treating anyone that came your way who was ugly, mean, or unkind the same way you would treat an animal you found caught in a trap. It would snarl at you if you approached and attempted to set it free, but only because it is wounded and scared. As the book *A Course in Miracles* puts it, "What people do is either an act of love, or a cry for love." [30] So as you adopt this expanded view and commit to not only act from love, but also Love What Comes in any situation, you open the door to a greater flow of abundance, because you have effectively alchemized the situation into an experience that inevitably yields benefit, sometimes in unexpected ways.

However, if all is one and love is all there is, then at some point in the eternally unfolding screenplay of existence, love would lose its luster and eventually become meaningless. You see, without the contrast of the dark, there can be no light, just like you can't have up without down, or hot without cold. So instead of fearing the darkness, what if we considered that it is actually a gift in disguise that allows us to not only experience the light, but also experience the joy of transmuting the darkness into light? What if you invited your demons to tea only to discover that they just needed a little sugar? By adopting this perspective, it allows us to see the value of life's shadows. If you think about it, you have never seen a beautiful work of art without shadows in it, have you? And your life is your soul's epic masterpiece! I firmly believe this is how all the great masters molded their own lives into masterpieces—by learning to Love What Comes. Or to quote John Lennon again, "Evolution and all hopes for a better world rest in the fearlessness and open-hearted vision of people who embrace life." We simply can't afford to run from fear any longer, it's time to embrace everything and rise.

IN THE EVENT OF A LOSS OF CABIN PRESSURE

During a flight, just prior to takeoff, the flight attendant instructs you that if the cabin should lose air pressure, always put on your own oxygen mask first, before assisting others. Similarly, if you want to not only survive, but abundantly thrive, I believe it is of paramount importance that you cultivate self-love first and foremost, because when we have love for ourselves, it is easier for us to courageously face our fears and Love What Comes. As humans, we have widely varied life purposes, but I believe the number one thing we are all here to unlock is self-love. Realize that you are your own soulmate, and self-love is the ultimate love story. And this realization starts by loving yourself exactly where you are and accepting that *you are perfectly imperfect*. A key ingredient to manifesting the abundance you deserve is feeling you are worthy of whatever you are asking for! And the truth is that a more divine creation than you has never been created, and it is time that you wake up and embrace the power of this realization. Self-loathing, self-judgment, and self-deprecation don't have a place in the future where you are headed. Those thoughts and ideas served you well in the past to provide contrast and lead you up to this point, but they were based in misunderstanding the true nature of the situation in which you find yourself. Esther Hicks is an inspirational speaker and author, who claims to channel Abraham – a group consciousness from the non-physical dimension – under the pseudonym Abraham-Hicks. Abraham-Hicks has said, "Appreciation and self-love are the most important aspects you could ever nurture. Appreciation of others and the appreciation of yourself are the closest vibrational matches to Source Energy of anything we have ever witnessed anywhere in this Universe." [21] What Abraham is proclaiming is that you are a divine being, one with the Source consciousness that creates and animates all things, and when you choose to step into self-love, you are aligning yourself with Source, allowing yourself to be open to the infinite gifts and abundance inherent within us all.

LET YOUR HEART OVERFLOW

In the book *The Untethered Soul*, author Michael Singer talks about the importance of maintaining an open heart, and he doesn't just mean figuratively. He suggests that our heart is essentially the energetic conduit through which life-force energy from Source flows. He also suggests that having an open heart is equivalent to having an open valve that allows in the abundant life-force energy that emanates from Source, and he goes on to say that most of us are unaware of how frequently we are opening and closing this valve. If we smell a familiar smell that reminds us of a good childhood memory, our hearts open. If someone says something we don't like, our hearts close. On and on we go all day, every day, opening and closing our precious hearts. It's like driving a Ferrari and switching back and forth between pushing the gas and the brake and then wondering why we aren't getting the optimal results out of our high-performance vehicle. Singer suggests that once we become aware of this process by which we receive energy from the infinitely abundant Source, we can then consciously choose to always leave our heart open. Over time, as you train yourself to maintain an open heart no matter what transpires, you become a vessel of overflowing universal love energy; you become like a cup that is spilling out the abundance of the Universe all around you. [32]

ATTITUDE OF GRATITUDE

When your heart is open, and the abundance of the Universe is flowing through you, you will begin to see the silver lining in every rain cloud. You will start to realize that every lump of coal you receive is really just a diamond in disguise waiting for you to apply the alchemical perspective necessary to transmute it into its highest potential. You become adept at training your eye to see the good in everything and to "see the light in others and treat them as if that is all you see," as Dr. Wayne Dyer once said. As a result, an attitude of gratitude naturally emerges as a byproduct of viewing your life through this much rosier lens. And gratitude is the doorway to attracting more of what we want to see in our world. On a physical level, tuning into joy and gratitude induces a somatic experience, which actually ripples these divine vibrations throughout your cells that not only positively affect you emotionally and spiritually, but also physically. Remember as a chip off the block of the Creator, the Creator and created rolled into one so to speak, whatever energy we are emanating we are creating and attracting more of into our life. So when we are in a state of appreciation or gratitude, we are calling in more experiences that our natural reaction is to be grateful for. If you want to unlock a better job, generate more money, or attract fulfilling relationships, then embracing where you are currently in your journey is the first step. Trust that you are exactly where you are meant to be. You aren't too late, and you aren't too early. You are exactly on time. Even if you don't prefer what is currently showing up in your life, realize it is much more about the attitude you bring than it is the details surrounding the given situation. Trust that you need the contrast of this experience to fully appreciate where you are headed next, and this is how you transmute and move through it. *What you resist persists; what you accept, you move through.*

GET TO THE ROOT OF THE MATTER

As we explore this idea of love, appreciation, and gratitude, consider your ancestors for a moment. In order for you to be born, an astronomical number of other souls had to exist first. Mainstream science estimates modern humans have been around for between two hundred to three hundred thousand years (and many believe we go back much further than that). However, if you go back just twelve generations over the last four hundred years or so, you have over four thousand grandparents! Think for a moment about how many difficulties, triumphs, hurts, loves, and losses had to transpire for you to arrive here in this now moment. For me personally, my grandfather, who was in the Navy and stationed at Pearl Harbor on December 7, 1941, is a great example. When his ship, The Utah, was bombed and ulti-mately sunk, he had to jump and swim for his life. If he hadn't made it out alive, like many of his shipmates, you would not be reading these words right now. The truth of the matter is, we are all so very loved that countless souls gave everything for us to be here now. The innumerable choice points, serendipities, and decisions that had to weave together like a perfectly woven tapestry for you to be here is truly breathtaking. Expand out this concept even further and consider that the heart of the Universe is conscious e-motion (energy in motion) and that it is still expanding and evolving, and up to this moment it has gone through approximately fourteen billion years of evolution to come to the point where it has evolved into you. So whenever you begin to doubt yourself, just remember that you're the tip of the evolutionary spear of a Universe that has sacrificed everything for you to exist!

THE GIFT OF FORGIVENESS

I believe we need to go back even farther than the creation of the Universe to truly understand the backstory of our existence and to trace love back to the root of its origins. The highly-official text I like to reference to fully understand humankind's origin story is a children's book written by Neale Donald Walsch titled *The Little Soul and the Sun*. In the book, the Sun is used as a metaphor for God, and the little soul, which represents us as humans, is one of infinite little lights that make up the entirety of the Sun. At the beginning, the little soul is blissfully floating in eternity experiencing the perfection of its exquisite existence, surrounded by a sea of other incredibly stunning lights. Then one day, a new thought occurs to the curious little soul: the idea of experiencing something besides bliss, love, and harmony. Ultimately the concept of forgiveness occurs to the little soul. So the soul begins a dialogue with the Sun expressing interest in experiencing forgiveness. All the other souls are fascinated by this dialogue transpiring between the little soul and the Sun as it is completely uncharted territory. Forgiveness, but what to forgive in this eternal perfection? The Sun goes on to ultimately say that he knew an adventurous little soul would eventually come up with something like this and that he indeed had a plan. It would require sending the soul to another place outside of perfection, followed by a second soul that would need to lower their vibration and dim their light so much that they would ultimately forget who and what they were and where they came from. Only then could the circumstances be created so that a horrible act, in need of forgiveness, could authentically be executed.

In the moment of the grand unveiling of the plan, a second brave little soul steps forward and says that he will play along and volunteer to lower his vibration and dim his light enough to do this horrible act, so that the first little soul can experience the gift of forgiveness. The second soul makes only one request of the first little soul: "In the moment that I strike you and smite you, in the moment that I do the worst to you that you could possibly imagine – in that very moment... Remember Who I Really Am." Because in the moment, his vibration will have been lowered so much so, that he will surely have forgotten himself, and if the first soul did not remember him, he may stay lost in a lower vibrational state for a very, very long time. I believe this is essentially humankind's origin story, and at various points in your evolution you have been both the first soul and the second soul, but as you read these words you are the first soul. I believe you were loved so very much that other souls stepped forward and lost themselves as a gift to you. Now it is your job to hold up your end of the bargain and see the light in others, especially those that have hurt you. See the light in others and treat them as if that is all you see. I strongly encourage any kids between the ages of one and one hundred and eleven to get *The Little Soul and the Sun*, to experience this beautiful story in its entirety. [39] There's a French expression that summarizes this beautiful lesson perfectly, "Tout comprendre c'est tout pardonner." To understand all is to forgive all.

THE NEW YOU

As you begin to flap your new butterfly wings, to let what comes, come, and to let what goes, go, floating through eternity admiring the exquisite perfection of the dance of life, relaxing into the innerstanding that everyone is always getting what they need to become the next greatest and grandest version of themselves, all close-minded judgments begin to melt away. Now that you hold the key to Love What Comes, and you innerstand that it is all happening for love regardless of how it looks on the surface, your life will begin to transform in miraculous ways. You will begin to unlock doors that were previously barred shut as you merge with your Higher Self, which is now further integrated and aligned with your physical being and seeing the world through your eyes. As a result, all of the gifts of manifestation and the infinite power of your Higher Self to alchemize every situation into a golden opportunity now become accessible to you as you step into the profound realization that *abundance is your birthright, the quintessence of your being.*

The Golden Key: Master the Youniverse

"You are the Universe experiencing itself." —Alan Watts

Once you alchemize and integrate the other seven keys in this book, the Golden Key to Master the Youniverse organically materializes to unlock your evolution and usher you into your natural state of unlimited abundance. Now what do I mean by the y-o-universe? Well, my favorite toys to play with as a child were *Masters of the Universe* characters, who fittingly live in a world called Eternia. Now all these years later as an adult, I have come to the realization that I came here to master the Universe—my own private youniverse. And that the key is to do so with a joyful, playful, child-like heart. Jesus had it right when he said, "Truly I tell you, unless you change and become like little children, you will never enter the kingdom of heaven." As I have proposed throughout this book, you are one with the Universe, not only physically, but also spiritually. However, it is even more personal and closer to home than you may have ever imagined. Alan Watts touched on how personal it truly is when he said, "What this is saying then is, that just as you don't know how you manage to be conscious, how you manage to grow and shape this body of yours, that doesn't mean to say that you're not doing it. Equally, you don't know how the Universe shines the stars, constellates the constellations and galactifies the galaxies, you don't know. But that doesn't mean to say that *you* aren't doing it in just the same way as you're breathing without knowing how you breathe." [42] How breathtaking it is to realize that we are the youniverse coming to know itself more fully with each passing moment.

A DREAM GOD ONCE HAD

You weren't created on the day you were born into physicality, just like you won't cease to exist when you are born back into the non-physical on the day of your death. The truth is that since you arrived here, you have simply had amnesia to who and what you were prior to your arrival. This reality is nothing more and nothing less than a dream God once had, and you are the dreamer and the dreamed rolled into one. It's the same as if you were to dream at night that a bear is chasing you through the woods. Then wake up in a sweat, grateful that the "real you" was safe, lying in bed dreaming; there was no bear all along. That's what is really going on in this simulated light show we call life on planet Earth, and it's time to wake up to the knowing that this is how God experiences herself throughout eternity — through you! You are God godding. We forget so that we can have the opportunity to remember, which makes it all new and exciting again.

RELATIVE TRUTHS

As we further explore what I mean by the term *you*niverse, it is important to innerstand that from an expanded view of reality, although oneness is the foundational truth that encompasses all truths, your *you*niverse is actually made up of relative truths: two apparently contradictory things that both hold true. In the *Conversations with God* book series, this is referred to as a "divine dichotomy". So truth is not strictly absolute; truth is determined in relation to the context in which we view it. For example, take the following statements: "You and I are separate." This is true. "You and I are one." This is also true. Both statements are true depending on the vantage point from which we are speaking. As we dissect the ultimate nature of reality, innerstanding these relative truths will also ensure your head doesn't swell up too big. Because, yes, you are God, however, so is the person next to you on the bus who is experiencing homelessness. God is it all. Whatever you name or point to, it is God. Nothing is outside of God. *We are all fractals of the one and* *only Source consciousness that creates and animates all things.* Think of Source like those Russian nesting dolls where a smaller replica is nested within each one of the larger versions. Each nested layer is a different vantage point or lens through which Source observes and experiences the vastness of existence and eternity, none of which is more valid or divine than any other vantage point, as every single one of them is necessary to make up the whole of creation and experience. When you truly begin to innerstand this truth, you realize *all judgment is self-judgment* because everywhere you go you are there waiting for yourself. In the Bible, God was having a dialogue with Moses when God said, "I am that, I am." You are what? THAT. And what is the root of THAT AM-ness? Consciousness. Source is simply what is left when forms or conceptualizations drop away. So when you drop the "THAT," "I AM" is all that remains, which is arguably the purest and truest name of God.

We are the architects of our reality, the lead director and actor in our own movie, the wizard hiding behind the curtain of our own private Oz, if you will. You can now laugh at the irony that you can achieve everything you've ever wanted, now that you realize you really don't need any of it! Because you are the one creating the story; you are the one writing the screenplay of your life. I often say the only thing I'm truly good at is spinning a good story. Every situation is neutral, and it is the story you spin that will dictate whether your experience will be positive or unpleasant. As you learn to Master the *You*niverse, you will become increasingly adept at crafting the best story, by seeing the light in others, and by realizing that your eternal divine beingness is the ultimate abundance. You will surrender to receive, knowing you're a divine being first and foremost–you are infinite abundance incarnate–and anything you achieve or attract into your world is just icing on the cake compared to this awe-inspiring truth. As we unpack this realization, that we are one with all of the abundance we see throughout the entire cosmos, it is important to explore the implications of this on our daily lives. The more we can innerstand these perspectives in a way that helps us bring it all down to Earth and ground it into our human selves, the more successfully we can navigate, harness, and ultimately unleash the abundance lying dormant within our human vessels.

EGGSTRAORDINARY

In 2009, Andy Weir wrote a now popular short story called "The Egg" that I believe comes close to explaining the core truth regarding how reality is structured. In the story, a recently deceased man that has transitioned to The Other Side is talking to God and she is explaining the ultimate nature of reality to him. She says, "I made this whole Universe for you. With each new life you grow and mature and become a larger and greater intellect." "Just me?" He asks, "What about everyone else?" To which she replies, "There is no one else, in this Universe, there's just you and me." God goes on to say, "Every time you victimized someone, you were victimizing yourself. Every act of kindness you've done, you've done to yourself. Every happy and sad moment ever experienced by any human was, or will be, experienced by you." Ultimately, God explains to the man that only after he has reincarnated and experienced every human life, will he have grown enough to be born, suggesting that essentially, the Universe—his *you*niverse—is simply his own personal egg.[43]

I envision the ultimate nature of reality to be similarly structured to the way Weir describes it. Prior to our exploration as individuated souls, I believe we are completely merged with Source consciousness—there is only one of us. At some point, the part of Source that is you decided to get adventurous and hatch off from the whole to experience something new, to see what it would be like to be a separate (relatively speaking) node of consciousness. A fractal of the whole, or chip off the block, if you will. And when you embarked on this soul journey sojourn, there were other souls that broke off from Source in close energetic proximity to where you separated from. Another way to envision this is if you think of Source as an infinite tree with infinite branches. No matter how mind-bogglingly infinite this tree of life happens to be, there are always going to be leaves or branches that are right next to each other blowing in the winds of eternity. And you could argue that the leaves next to you are more closely related to you than those far away on the other side of the tree, the same way you could say your fingers are more closely related to each other than they are to your toes. Yet ultimately, it's still all one tree, or one body.

Another one of my favorite interviewees I've had on *The Positive Head Podcast* [1], former Harvard neurosurgeon and author of the *New York Times* best-selling book *Proof of Heaven* [2], Dr. Eben Alexander, explains that during his harrowing near-death experience he was shown how we repeatedly reincarnate here in this "soul school" called Earth. Each of us has a close-knit soul group that is made of the same souls that appear in our Earthly life movies time and time again. We embark on the journey of physicality together with our soul family with the aim of playing the necessary roles for one another, to help each other evolve and reach our divine potential in a setting that is more conducive to stimulate growth than the perfection from whence we came. And we return again and again, to continually refine ourselves, within and across lifetimes. In essence, God is the all-pervading, ever-expanding consciousness, that infinitely fractalizes and evolves himself through all living things. He is the oak tree hidden in every acorn awaiting the right conditions to emerge into its full glory, and our soul groups are the perfect soil to create those conditions. Source's eternal self-love story truly is the greatest romance ever written.

ROLL WITH THE ROLES

There are many souls who have played, or continue to play, important roles in my own life who have interesting connections to my birthday, July 28th. I could fill a short book with all the synchronicities that continue to unfold surrounding my birthday, but for now I will just share a few to highlight my point. I believe myself and these souls make up a part of my close-knit soul group that has repeatedly chosen to reincarnate together so that we may aid in each other's evolution. The synchronicities relating to my birthday are an affirmation to me that these souls are in fact close reflections that I should pay special attention to. Consider first, the significance of July 28th on the paternal side of my family. My father was 28 when I was born on his birthday, July 28th. His grandmother (my great-grandmother) was also born on July 28th, and her mother (my great-great-grandmother) passed away on July 28th. Similar to me, my father is extremely passionate about his spirituality, however in his case, it is in a much more closed-minded, fear-based Conservative Christian context. I consider that perhaps there was another now when I already played the role of my current father Roger, and at that time another soul closely related to me was experiencing the avatar of Brandon.

Or consider a former close friend and business partner. Both his child's mother and grandmother share my birthday. Through this partnership, I experienced the greatest betrayal (i.e., something to forgive) of my life. However, I consider that perhaps I have already sat on that side of the table where I played that particular "villain" character, which interestingly enough Dr. Eben Alexander says are often the souls we are closest to on The Other Side. From this expanded view, one might say there has never been a victim in all of eternity, rather *it's all just spiritual business* and soul contracts being divinely honored.

Or when I think about the communal property I call the Mystic Manor that I established in 2019, I consider the dozens of colorful characters that have been a vital part of making it what it is. Including one, who also shares my birthday, who has been both the most challenging character at some points, and the most helpful at others. And at times, he has been an uncanny and obvious reflection of challenging aspects of my own character that I've continually worked to improve; he has triggered those less desirable aspects of myself, bringing them to the surface for further healing. When I consider some of these other close reflections, I sometimes ponder the idea that perhaps I have already played every character in the house — from my own partner Karen, to my roommate with the name Brandon, to the housekeeper (who happens to remind me of my grandmother) — which has now led to me being in the role of the steward of the spaceship (as I like to refer to myself, since the property looks like a spaceship). Or who knows, perhaps my character is the beginning point and Dora, the joyous housekeeper, is the most evolved experience to be had at the Mystic Manor. Who can say for sure? The point is, when you start considering the concept that you have already played (or will play) every role in existence to experience all the possible vantage points, it begins to sink in that all judgment is self-judgment, and that the amount we judge truly is equivalent to the amount of ignorance we hold. In reality, all judgment is the absence of love and love is the absence of judgment.

The ultimate aim of our journey is to play infinite roles and to evolve over time. I believe when you finish this life and get to The Other Side, where you are in your development is assessed and that determines what avatar, or human character story arc, is a close enough vibrational match for you to "drop into" and experience next. And this doesn't necessarily mean in the linear future either. You may get to The Other Side and have the option to be a samurai from the year 1300 or a science officer from the year 3188. I believe we are every human who has ever been, or will be. Eternity provides us with infinite runway to try on countless costumes so that we may get a well-rounded experience of all reality. In Wier's short story "The Egg", God says, "You play Hitler, and everyone he kills. You play Jesus, and everyone who follows him." As challenging as this may be to fathom, I believe it to be true. What we are is not for the faint of heart. It is said by some that those souls who choose to embark into physicality are highly respected and among the bravest to dare experience such extreme separation from Source. But remember, there's nothing to fear because from the most expanded view *it's all happening for love.*

FREE WILL AND DESTINY

One of the most useful ways I have found to tap into my innate potential to Master the *You*niverse is to navigate my life from the perspective that *our lives play out at the corner of free will and destiny*. Early on I explained how time is an illusion and that your fifth birthday party is happening on another channel right now, you simply aren't tuned into it. Your future birthday party is also happening on another channel right now that you are also not tuned into in this now moment. If we innerstand this, it is relatively easy for us to conceptualize that everything is destined because it is all happening in the eternal now. But then how can we experience free will? Source is infinitely abundant in both time and energetic resources, and so your Higher Self is playing out every potential that your human avatar could possibly experience, simultaneously on infinite timelines. And you have free will to choose which version of your character you want to experience this time around.

Much like in the movie *The Matrix Reloaded* — Neo meets with the Architect and sees many other versions of himself playing out on the TV screens and realizes other versions of his character have been here before. Or when I was in college and had my first psychic reading one day in Atlanta, Georgia. The intuitive woman looked at me and said, "I see you living in a cold place like Chicago working in business." My jaw hit the floor because at that time I was planning to move to Chicago and work with my uncle's business that was headquartered there! Then she looked at me and said, "But there is a totally different path for you in music." At that time I had never made music of any kind. However, about a year later, I got inspired to form a band. Shortly after forming my band, I went to another psychic, who said that I would move to California to pursue music. Not long after, I met someone with music business connections in California who insisted my band and I should be based there, and after visiting with him, we decided to permanently relocate across the country from Nashville to California.

So what I believe the initial psychic in Atlanta was seeing was the two potential Brandon's most likely to manifest based on where I was vibrationally at the moment I was sitting in front of her. When you start to consider any possibility for yourself, it is important to realize that no matter how grandiose what you are imagining may seem, if you can imagine it, Source has been there, done that, and gotten the t-shirt. In fact, your Higher Self is so infinite, it can experience anything you are dreaming up and even things you haven't yet thought of. And this is the abundance that is now accessible for you to tap into.

ON THE BACKS OF GIANTS

It has been said that when the student is ready, the master will appear. A master or teacher that you attract into your life may appear in many forms. Perhaps as a person, or in the form of a book, podcast, online workshop, or some other avenue. Regardless of who and how, if the teacher is legitimate, they will always point you to the same truth: *you have the power.* This is exactly what many masters throughout history—such as Jesus, Buddha, and Lau Tzu—were teaching. This is also what Adam figured out in the *Masters of the Universe* cartoons when he would level up and morph into the superhuman He-Man by proclaiming, "I have the power!" Unfortunately, the teachings of masters have often been hijacked and misconstrued by those who wished to control others. Ironically, because these misguided leaders never fully understood the teachings themselves, they acquired a lesser level of power than the authentic power they could have accessed.

If you examine the teachings of these masters, without the lens of those that misinterpreted or manipulated their message, you can clearly see how many of the great spiritual or religious teachings are actually quite aligned with the concepts limned within these pages. Since Jesus is essentially The Beatles of spiritual teachers, let's use him as an example and analyze a few of his quotes. Consider the following: "Very truly I tell you, whoever believes in me will do the works I have been doing, and they will do even greater things than these." This is essentially another way of saying, "You have the power," as he is stating that your potential is equal to or even greater than his own powerful, awe-inspiring works. Or when Jesus said, "I and the Father are one," he was referring to oneness. Or in the quote I referenced earlier — "If you have faith as small as a mustard seed, you can say to this mountain, 'Move from here to there,' and it will move." — he was teaching the Law of Attraction. And when a group who were casting stones at him said, "We are not stoning you for any good work, but for blasphemy, because you, a mere man, claim to be God." And he replied, "Is it not written in your Law, 'I have said you are gods'?" Jesus was agreeing that yes, he is God, but so are you! It's time to drop the idea that Jesus required worship, because the truth is he never asked to be put on a pedestal. In fact, he was more interested in service, such as in the well-known story in which he washed his disciples' feet. In essence, he was putting *you* on the pedestal, and continually delivering insights to empower you to Master the *You*niverse.

Many other great masters were also teaching these same truths in various ways. If you wade through all the dogma and get to the core teaching that ties together all of the world's largest religions such as Christianity, Judaism, Buddhism, Hinduism, Islam, Zoroastrianism, Taoism, and Confucianism, they all teach what is known as the Golden Rule: Do unto others as you would have them to do unto you. Why is this rule crucial and golden? Because as we have stated, there are no others. All is one and you are always doing it to self! As Rumi so eloquently said it, "In fact, my soul and yours are the same, you appear in me, I in you, we hide in each other." [27] This is why we receive what we give. This is why service is the path to true abundance.

As you move more fully into your own mastery, you realize that a master also embraces whatever shows up because you know you have not only co-created it with your Higher Self, but it is always put on your path to lead you to the next greatest and grandest version of yourself. Whatever is arising and transpiring is always exactly what you need to sharpen your axe of consciousness so to speak. Especially when something challenging arises, it is important for us to remember that smooth seas never made for a skilled sailor, and we all came here to become master manifesters and skilled sailors as we sail upon the seas of eternity.

CREATE YOUR MASTERPIECE

I believe the art of manifestation is the next great art form to be highly valued and revered on this planet, and that anyone drawn to this book and content like it is meant to become one of the great heARTists that usher in the new world by always, in all ways, living from a love-centered place. Now that you have begun to innerstand the reality that *you are the only one in the room* and everyone is a prop in your own private movie, that *everywhere you go you're there waiting for yourself,* that there are no others, and that your life plays out at the corner of free will and destiny, you have laid the necessary groundwork to utilize the Golden Key to Master the *You*niverse. And as it sinks in that you are so abundant that you created everything that you see — every star in the sky, all the abundance on this and all the planets in the *you*niverse — you will realize that all the hardships of the world are in some way, shape, or form a reflection of your consciousness, and you can begin to own and accept all of it, knowing that it is self-created and that you have been the one hiding behind the curtain of creation all along. By doing so, you become empowered to help alchemize all the challenges that the world is destined to overcome.

You are moving from victimhood to conscious creatorship and mastery. You can now look around and see something you like and say, "I did that," and also see something you don't like and say, "I did that, too." You can playfully navigate through life with a childlike heart, maintaining the core intention to learn and grow from any missteps. Statistical probabilities of how likely it is that you accomplish this or that become nothing more than white noise, because of course you make it, you are the only one here! *It's always this or something better.* You realize just like in the movies when the hero hits a low point, it isn't over if you haven't won yet, and all your "challenges" are really just blessings in disguise for you to have the joyous experience of overcoming! You are the Master of the *You*niverse.

A STELLAR SIGN OF ABUNDANCE

As we step into our childlike selves and take on a more trusting, carefree approach to life, I believe it is important to find ways to play with the *you*niverse, which is why I am going to suggest a super exciting and abundance-validating way to do so together in a moment. Before I do, I would like to share a magical story to show you how abundance can begin to flow when you open your heart, have faith in the *you*niverse, and say yes to life by choosing to play. I originally met Vajra, the co-creator of the cover art on this book, a few years ago, when he was live-painting a stunning piece portraying a being known as the Demiurge that has been described as an artisan-like figure, rooted in Platonic philosophy, responsible for fashioning and maintaining the physical Universe — essentially the artistic being credited for the creation of the cosmos. Sounds a bit familiar eh, perhaps a self-portrait? Synchronistically, this live-painting was happening at an event produced by my friend Christopher David Jackson called A-Bun-Dance. When I first saw the Demiurge, I was so blown away by the benevolent power and beauty of the almost-completed work that I told Vajra I was interested in buying it. A few days later we talked on the phone and he told me that he would sell the Demiurge piece to me for $7,777. At that time I had not purchased much art, and certainly had never paid $7,777 for anything that could be deemed so impractical. However, I really loved the piece. And because I innerstand the reality that money is only an energetic currency that is meant to flow (as implied by its name), I knew that if the intentions and dynamics of the transaction were pure and positive, which indeed they were, then me buying this painting would ultimately unlock more abundance for us both.

So I decided to agree to his price with one condition: if he would be willing to allow me to make monthly payments to him over a few years. He replied that he would, but only if he could give me a print of the Demiurge and delay giving me the original painting until my payments were made in full over those few years. I told him that I really wanted the original while making payments as that would feel the best to me energetically. He went on to explain to me that he had been burned in a similar situation in the past and didn't feel comfortable trusting me with the original painting prior to me having paid it off. After respectfully sharing with him that I believed his choice to operate from fear instead of love and trust in this situation would actually have the opposite effect of protecting him and would ultimately lead to a lack of abundance, I was still not able to convince him to trust me enough to allow me to take possession of the Demiurge painting before paying it off.

So as a last-ditch effort, I decided to invite him to play a game with the *you*niverse. I explained to him that sometimes when I was unsure about the best course of action to take in a situation, I would ask the *you*niverse for a sign. Typically, I will proclaim that if I see or hear X before date Y then I will take it as a sign to do Z. Example: if I randomly hear someone talk about India in the next forty-eight hours then I will take that as a sign that I should accept a recent invitation to attend a retreat there. If I don't hear about India in that time frame, then I won't go. I explained to him that I have seen some wild results playing this game with the *you*niverse in the past. And I suggested he may want to consider asking the *you*niverse for a sign that I am trustworthy, and that selling me the painting under my terms would result in a positive experience. He half-heartedly said he would consider playing the game and we said our goodbyes.

I didn't really expect to hear from him again. However, Vajra did decide to try my idea, although his ask from the *you*niverse was fairly out of this world. Since the Demiurge he painted is quite cosmic looking, he decided to state that the grandiose sign he would need in order to feel comfortable honoring my terms would be to see an Unidentified Flying Object (UFO) within two weeks. At that time, he had witnessed one UFO sighting in his life and had always wanted to experience seeing another one. Well the two weeks passed without him seeing any UFOs or little green men, so he forgot about our potential deal. However, about three weeks later, he was booked to live-paint at an event called Disclosure Fest that was focused around disclosing UFO phenomena. During the event, many people actually saw a UFO, including Vajra. He immediately thought of the Demiurge sign request he had made, but since more than two weeks had passed, technically the sign occurred outside of the parameters of the game, and so he still wasn't entirely convinced to sell me the painting.

Now unbeknownst to us both, we had a close mutual friend named Shane. I was at Shane's house the day before Disclosure Fest and he showed me an art print he was about to buy and I said, "That looks like the same artist I was recently trying to buy art from." So I showed him a picture of the Demiurge and we confirmed it was indeed the same artist, Vajra. I explained to Shane that Vajra didn't take my offer to make payments over time and Shane went on to say that he knew Vajra very well and would put in a good word for me. So at Disclosure Fest the next day, Shane happened to run into Vajra, which led to a conversation where Shane expressed to him that I am extremely trustworthy and recommended that he sell me the Demiurge painting. So even though the UFO timing was a bit off, the fact that Shane vouched for me on the same day that he witnessed the UFO, Vajra took that as a close enough sign to take my offer.

After Disclosure Fest, Vajra reached out to me to tell me he wanted to move forward with selling me the Demiurge painting after all. Now where it gets really interesting is what opened up in both of our lives because he was willing to be playful with the *you*niverse, Trust the Mystery, and open his heart and mind. First, it led to us becoming great friends. Then when I set up the Mystic Manor, it led to him helping to make it abundant with art by curating and creating one of the world's first visionary art galleries there. And when I began booking guests for my new talk show *Optimystic*, I invited him to not only be the first visionary artist guest on Episode One, but to also help me book all the other visionary artists, since he is so well connected in that world. Completely by random, I also booked the singer Imagika Om on Episode One as my first musical guest. Because of this "random" booking, Imagika Om and Vajra connected on the show for the first time that night and fell sanely in love, and ended up getting married at the Mystic Manor four months later!

The reality is, had I not been willing to pay top dollar for visionary art and allow my monetary currency to flow, I would not have opened up an abundant wave of significant value that Vajra ultimately brought into my life by artifying the Mystic Manor, connecting me with so many great artists for *Optimystic*, co-creating the stellar cover art on this book, not to mention forming what has developed into a very close friendship. Had I not been willing to follow my heart and intuition by allowing my currency to flow toward something that many would deem as frivolous, my currency may have remained stagnant and I think it is unlikely those same dollars used elsewhere could have possibly yielded experiences as enriching. And had he not been willing to overcome his fear of loss and move into a state of childlike playfulness as I suggested he do with the game with the *you*niverse, he would not have stepped into a timeline where he unlocked the abundance of our friendship and the deep fulfillment he gets from being involved with the Mystic Manor and *Optimystic*. Not to mention, he would not have connected with the woman who is now the love of his life and wife! Luckily for the both of us, he chose to step into his role as the Master of his *You*niverse. And now that you are on the path to become the Master of your *You*niverse and begin your eternal dance with a-bun-dance, I would like to invite you to play a game with the *you*niverse to unlock the infinite abundance that is your birthright.

Care to Play a Game with the *You*niverse?

Now that the genie is out of the bottle, there is only one thing to do from here on out: play away for eternity! Tap into the ONEderFULL vibration of celebration by remembering that abundance is not only your natural state, but also the birthright you are being beckoned to re-member. It is your destiny to eternally play among the cosmic fields as the star of the *you*niverse that you truly are, and I would like to start off this exciting new chapter of your next now moment by extending an invitation for us to co-create and play together. The game and exercises I am about to explain are intended to yield powerful results for you sometime within the next 88 days. Keep in mind that this game is designed to demonstrate your powerful abundance manifestation abilities over a relatively short period of time so that you get excited, inspired and accustomed to playing with the *you*niverse in this way for the rest of your life!

STEP ONE

So to kick off this abundance-generating game with the *you*niverse, I want you to take a moment to close your eyes, and ask yourself: If you had to quantify it, what is the monetary value of this book to you? What do you feel is the honest value of the Golden Key you now hold in your pocket? And more importantly, how much abundance do you wish to cultivate in your life? Because now, I am inviting you to go to goldenkey.gift to make a monetary contribution for any amount you choose. For whatever currency amount you opt to flow into this game, we are going to set the co-creative intention that it will act as a seed that will sprout and multiply into greater abundance for you within the next 88 days. So don't just choose a number based on what your brain tells you is a "reasonable" amount. Instead, authentically ask in your heart what currency amount will feel like a mutually rewarding energetic exchange. I encourage you to perhaps push yourself a little bit out of your comfort zone, and choose a contribution amount that allows you the experience of generosity, without completely breaking your bank of course. Because as much as I want you to stretch yourself energetically in every way with this game (for both of our sakes), please don't get evicted in the process, because I only have so much room on my couch! I just want to give you the opportunity to create a feeling of abundance within yourself by choosing to spend money when you really aren't required to. And keep in mind, the financial contribution amount is relative. It is safe to say that for the vast majority of you, contributing $50 would be a bigger energetic stretch than the richest man in the world, Jeff Bezos, contributing $500,000. So, it is less about the exact dollar amount you choose, and more about tapping into a feeling of being intentionally generous with your offering, which is the spark that catalyzes abundance to generously flow back to you!

One of the other main reasons I am giving you the option to monetarily contribute to this game is to give you an opportunity to take action to demonstrate to the *you*niverse that you are ready to begin your journey toward unlocking infinite abundance, by picking up the First Key—See the Oneness—and turning it in its lock. The separation between us is an illusion. I am you, and you are me. Everything you do, you do to yourself. This is why this counterintuitive approach—giving in order to receive—works, because any amount you give, you are essentially giving to yourself. So then the question becomes, what do you think you are worth? How much do you feel you deserve and how willing and receptive are you to receive? Whenever you choose to give more than is required of you in this life, you are consciously choosing to tune into the higher frequency of abundance. And since reality always mirrors back the vibrations we put out, you will be attracting more abundance into your life by doing so! This is why the famous saying, "You get what you give," is such a powerful universal truth. I like to say, "You get what you give, and then some!"

Regardless of the amount that you chose, set the intention for your contribution to act as the symbolic marker and catalyst for the amount of abundance you wish to unlock in your life. Some of you may find your contribution amount flows back to you threefold, sevenfold, or even tenfold through some unforeseen currency stream, similar to what occurred for Dr. Bruce Lipton in the mind-blowing story I'm about to share. Others of you may attract a new fulfilling relationship, or see major improvements in your health. Still others may find your schedule shifts to allow you more time to focus on doing what you love. There's really no limit to the varied ways abundance can manifest in your movie. In the coming pages, you will be guided through several simple yet powerful exercises to help you catalyze these real, tangible results. Abundance can come in a myriad of forms, so be sure to keep your eyes, ears, and heart open, with a sense of healthy expectation and detachment. And as you and the other readers play this game, magical stories of synchronicity and abundance will inevitably unfold. And at goldenkey.gift, you will have the opportunity to share your results as well as see the inspiring results of others.

Also, since you know the importance of where you choose to align your energy and intentions, I feel it is imperative to let you know that my primary intention with the currency I receive from this game is to use it to bring more consciousness-elevating material and media to the world. Flashy sports cars never really did it for me anyway! And as I mentioned at the beginning, I intend to practice what I preach when I say we should let currency flow when it is attached to an intention that is positive and pure, because I sincerely believe that's how it comes back to us manyfold. This is why, when you opt to play the game at goldenkey.gift, you will automatically be registered as a *key master*. As a *key master*, you will receive 50% of the revenue generated from anyone who you share your personal free book download code with who also decides to play this game with the *you*niverse (further details at goldenkey.gift). Helping you to unlock more financial abundance in this way is the good kind of selfish, because *if you win, I win.* Besides, this isn't just my information in this book, it's ours, and I want you to be inspired to share it with the other you's and me's out there who really need and are ready to receive it. This game is meant to be a fun way to cultivate mutual abundance, by spreading the wisdom of these keys and inviting as many people as possible to flow abundant energy into this game with the *you*niverse. Just as the butterfly spreads pollen between plants, you will be spreading empowering wisdom and seeds of abundance to anyone you choose to share your code with, and the natural byproduct will be more monetary energy and golden experiences for allLOVEus to share. Indeed it's true, *a rising tide raises all ships.*

So again, if you haven't already made your monetary contribution at goldenkey.gift, go do so now to get the currency flowing. In the moment you are consciously choosing to pay for something you aren't required to spend money on, sit back and take a moment to notice how amazing and empowered you feel. That's the wonderful vibration of abundance that you have drummed up within yourself, which is the first ripple of currency flowing outward from you which will ultimately grow into a swelling wave that inevitably comes crashing back upon your own shores.

STEP TWO

Next, ask yourself what form(s) of abundance you would most like to unlock over the next 88 days and beyond. Here are a few foundational forms to consider:

Physical Healing
Mental/Emotional Healing
Monetary/Financial/Wealth
Fulfilling Relationship
Friendship
Meaningful Experience

Support
Free Time
Travel
Peace/Happiness/Joy
Career/Employment
Hobbies/Talents
Knowledge/Wisdom
Perception/Intuition

You may choose one or multiple of the aforementioned forms of abundance, or any other form you come up with on your own. Take a moment now to really feel into what it is that you desire. What are you seeking most? What do you want to experience more of in your life? Take your time. I recommend sitting in a quiet place, away from any noise or distractions. Close your eyes. Take a few, deep breaths to help you become more aware of your body and focus inward. Now imagine yourself as the greatest and grandest version of you. What does that feel like? What is this ideal version of yourself doing? What are you wearing? Where are you? Are there others with you, or are you alone? Allow yourself to be playful and open your imagination so that the vision that wants to flow through, can flow through. The answers that come to you will give you clues as to the form(s) of abundance that your soul is most craving. Do this exercise with an open mind and heart. Try not to judge what you think or what you see. When you allow your imagination to carry you in this way, you are gleaning a unique glimpse into the joyful quintessence of your being, which is home to all of the abundance which you seek.

STEP THREE

Now that you have a clearer vision of the form(s) of abundance which you wish to unlock, it's time to pluck your manifestation desires from the ethers. Write them down on paper, or document them in some other way. Think of this as the first exciting step toward them beginning to manifest physically. You may be wondering how detailed you should be in this written expression of your desires. You should be as detailed or as general as feels right to you. Both approaches are valid and will lead to an influx of abundance, as long as your intentions remain positive and pure.

If you opt to go for a more detailed manifestation approach, I recommend setting specific intention(s) for whatever details are most important to you, such as: I intend to manifest a new job with these specific hours, this level of pay, doing this type of work. I intend to manifest **X** amount of financial abundance. I intend to attract a fulfilling new relationship within the next **X** months with a partner who possesses **X** attributes.

Dr. Bruce Lipton shared an epic example of this type of specific manifestation approach when he was on Episode 161 of *The Positive Head Podcast*.[24] In the story he shared multiple synchronicities that wove together in fascinating ways, one of which involved a pivotal part of his journey self-publishing *The Biology of Belief*.[23] He was put in a position in which he needed to very quickly manifest $30,000 to put toward book printing in order to capitalize on a series of fortuitous events which led to Amazon highlighting his book in national newspapers in honor of their ten year anniversary. So his wife, Margaret, proceeded to do a series of abundance manifestation exercises, including speaking to the Universe, explicitly stating what she was calling in, much like you are doing in this step. They trusted that because the underlying intention of the book was to spread empowering information, abundance would flow to them, in the form they were requesting or something better. Within one week Margret received an unexpected letter informing her that a building she had bought shares in 15 years prior, but had not thought about in many years, had been sold, and she would soon receive a large check for her portion of the sale. When they learned the amount they would receive they were ecstatic because it was 10x what they had asked for: $300,000! This is a great example of, "You get what you give, and then some," when you're in alignment with your purpose and have a pure intention to benefit others.

Alternatively, you can remain more general in your intentions. Since we can't always see the big picture in the same way our Higher Self can, sometimes it's best not to be too worried about the specifics and instead focus on the underlying experience we hope to achieve from whatever we are wishing to attract.

Here's an example: perhaps instead of being super specific and saying, "I want to meet a man that is at least 6' tall with olive skin and brown eyes who is between the ages of 30 and 32 years old," ask yourself: What is the underlying experience that you are seeking from manifesting a new partner with this description? Is it really crucial that this person be 6' tall, or at a deeper level is it a fulfilling connection which you are truly seeking, and you just like the idea of having it happen with someone that you feel comfortable wearing high heels around? If you indeed manifest this person and they turn out to be a total jerk, you may be better off just wearing flats! Remember, there are infinite ways the *youni*verse can fulfill your core desires. So that's why in many cases I recommend being general and only focus on the foundational forms of abundance you wish to manifest, because if your intentions are positive and pure, then your Higher Self will gladly fill in the details!

Whether you choose to be more detailed or more general, write it down. You may record just one or a few words, or you may fill an entire piece of paper documenting your desires. There is no wrong way to do this. Just allow whatever wants to come through, to flow through. Once you have the forms of abundance that you are calling in documented, read them out loud repeatedly, and revisit them regularly over the next 88 days to continue vibrationally anchoring them into your world. Lastly, to help anchor them in even further, it's important to drum up and amplify the vibration of abundance regularly by implementing the key word in the Law of Attraction – inspired, disciplined *action*! So now I will share three simple yet powerful exercises to help you consistently drum up the vibration of abundance that you have begun tapping into.

The Rich-U-All Action Plan

Keep in mind, in regards to the exercises I am about to explain, I believe you will get out what you put into this, as my grandmother said. The more energy you put into the following exercises, the more abundance you will manifest as a result of performing them.

To aid in unlocking this new flow of abundance, we are going to participate in a collective abundance ritual (Rich-U-All) to help you tap into your manifestation powers. According to Oxford Languages, *ritual* is defined as "a solemn ceremony consisting of a series of actions performed according to a prescribed order." I see rituals simply as any planned energetic actions and intentions we put our focus on that then essentially give us a "permission slip," as the spiritual teacher Bashar[3] refers to it, to help our brains rationalize and reconcile our immense manifestation abilities. Basically all you need is a good excuse to allow yourself to flex your manifestation muscles. So this game with the *you*niverse abundance spell you're casting is designed as a simple demonstration of how letting currency flow forth from you when it is connected to something as positive and well-intended as this game, ultimately doesn't cost you anything from the most expanded view point, because it actually unlocks more abundance for allLOVEus. This is how we create more abundance in the world—by aligning with love-centric endeavours, because love is the only resource that isn't reduced or diluted when given away, rather it expands and creates more of itself by multiplying!

Now that you've made your energetic contribution to this game at goldenkey.gift and let your monetary currency flow, here are the next steps you are going to take to playfully allow and invite even more abundance to flow back into your reality! As I previously mentioned, there are no must-do's with this Rich-U-All Action Plan. As an infinitely abundant, highly creative creator, feel free to modify any parts of this ritual as you see fit. There are infinite ways to unlock that which you seek to manifest.

Here are the three exercises of the Rich-U-All Action Plan. For optimal results, I recommend performing all three of these exercises at least once a day for the next 88 days:

1) **Recite Your Mantra:** Right when you wake up and right when you go to sleep, or at any point during your day, stop whatever you are doing and emphatically and repeatedly recite this mantra 8 times: "I AM infinite abundance, I AM that which I seek." If you choose to create the time, do multiple rounds, but always in intervals of 8 (e.g., 16, 24, 36, etc.). I recommend doing 64 (8 rounds of 8). It is important that you don't just say the mantra. Focus your attention with the intention to really feel the mantra in your heart, mind and soul as you recite it. In your mind's eye, imagine yourself already having the forms of abundance you are attracting. Hold on to that vision, and feel what it would feel like in every cell of your being to already be experiencing the abundance that is your birthright. Feeling is the bridge that energetically leads us to the vibrational pools of abundance, and you want to flood your body with these potent vibrations.

   o **Focus on the Key:** At goldenkey.gift you can order a physical Golden Key necklace, like the one on the cover of this book, that is made with real gold. Be sure to always wear it so that you can hold and focus on it as a physical symbol of the abundance you're unlocking while you are reciting your daily mantra. If you didn't order one or haven't received your real Golden Key in the mail yet, you can also alchemize any ordinary key into your Golden Key with the power of your imagination and intention. By focusing on a physical symbol or representation of the Golden Key, you further ground in the permission slip to call in more abundance. Imagine your key as an "abundance generator" that will imbue and exude the energy of health, wealth, peace, prosperity, and whatever other form(s) of abundance you are calling in. View your magical "abundance generator" through the eyes of your excited inner child who is longing to come out and play — the inner child who could have easily and effortlessly jumped into an empty cardboard box, and with their potent imagination transformed it into a spaceship and experienced all of the sensations that allowed them to feel like they were actually whisking through the cosmos. The truth is your inner child is longing to come out and playfully lead you into your dream-come-true reality. This is their domain, invite them to come out and lead you. Every time you look at or touch your Golden Key, set the intention to see it as the physical evidence of the expanding abundance stream that has already begun flowing into your life.

o **Retrain Your Brain:** I also strongly encourage you to download the free Golden Key wallpaper for your phone and/or tablet device at goldenkey.gift and set it as your lock screen image. Train yourself to recite your mantra every time you unlock your device(s). Most of us unlock our digital devices dozens of times a day. By capitalizing on this frequent action, we are constantly navigating ourselves back into the vibration of abundance. This will help to retrain your brain to remain in this elevated state.

2) **Breathe It All In:** When you combine the words "birth" and "death" together, you get "breath" — our sacred connection to Source. We are birthed into the next now moment with each new breath and we

experience a mini-death with each exhale. The more you practice connecting to your breath, the greater your connection between your mind, body, and spirit will become. For this next exercise, at least once a day, practice consciously breathing in the vast abundance of the *you*niverse. The rule of three for survival suggests that humans can typically go about three weeks without food, three days without water, and three minutes without air. Oxygen is the most abundant element on Earth, and the only one that is still completely free to everyone on our planet. Yet most people tend to breathe very shallow, which is a reflection of their disconnection from abundance. So with this exercise, you are going to take a few moments to intentionally inhale and exhale through your mouth in order to flood every cell of your body with an abundance of oxygen as a symbol of the expanded abundance you are stepping into in your life. Simply extend your arms directly in front of you, palms facing upwards, ready to receive. On an inhale, retract your arms into your chest, while simultaneously closing your hands to make fists, in a quick pulling action toward your heart. On an exhale, return your arms to the original position, arms extended in front with palms facing up. On each inhale, imagine you're pulling abundance into your being based on the intentions that you have set. Focus on the inhale and just allow yourself to exhale naturally as you find your rhythm. Breathe deeply as you close your hands and pull them into your chest, remembering that this abundance of oxygen is a reflection of the abundance you are calling into your life. You can also playfully imagine details of the intentions you have set. Perhaps you picture yourself in the house of your dreams, as the healthiest and most peaceful version of yourself, in a highly-fulfilling relationship or career, but always with a healthy sense of detachment to the details knowing that it will manifest as "this or something better" and will always arrive in divine timing. As you practice and find a circular rhythm, repeat this process while breathing at a rate that is comfortable for you, and for as long as feels good to you (I recommend 88-second cycles). On the last inhale, hold your breath in for as long as you possibly can, while focusing on in-joying the abundance you will most certainly feel tingling and circulating through every cell in your body. When you can hold no longer, release with a forceful exhale, as you imagine that you are releasing any old limiting beliefs and energy back to the *you*niverse to be transmuted and alchemized into abundance. I recommend repeating this cycle at least 3 times, although any amount will give you benefit. You can also combine this exercise with the first one by reciting your mantra silently to yourself while you are pulling in abundance.

3) **A-Bun-Dance:** At least once a day I also encourage you to get up, move your body, and do the a-bun-dance! Martha Graham said, "Dance is the hidden language of the soul," [16] and the more you can step into the frequency of joy in the now moment and celebrate all the magnificent glory it entails, as well as the inevitability of more abundance flowing into your life, the quicker it will manifest, because you're being it to see it! Like the Native American artist Supaman said, "They say to dance like nobody is watching. I think that implies that we are afraid or ashamed to dance in front of the people. I say dance like everybody is watching. Dance like your children are watching, your ancestors, your family. Dance for those who are hurting, those who can't dance, those who lost loved ones and those who suffer injustices throughout the world. Let every step be a prayer for humanity! Most of all dance for the Creator, who breathed into your soul so you may celebrate this gift of life!"[34] So put on your favorite song and do the a-bun-dance and watch how quickly this fun exercise will elevate your vibration. A great example of a song I recommend listening to while doing the a-bun-dance is called "Painting (Masterpiece)" by

Lewis Del Mar [11], because it speaks to our ability as heARTists to paint the life of our dreams!

As you play, remember to let your inner child lead and be sure to not take any of the exercises too seriously, and feel free to improvise if you would like. You are already a raging success just for saying yes to inviting more playfulness into your life by taking the initiative and action to play this game with the *you*niverse! Once again, there is no definitive right or wrong way to do these exercises. The most important thing is your intention and that you are "feeling it" and having fun. If you are disciplined and stick with this Rich-U-All Action Plan for at least 88 days I can assure you that you will achieve stellar results, or your karma back guaranteed! I say at least 88 days, because I strongly encourage you to use these exercises indefinitely to continually tap into your powerful abundance manifestation abilities for the rest of your life. Also, be sure to visit goldenkey.gift to report your inSPIRITional results, so that we can all benefit, enjoy and celebrate in your success.

I believe once we awaken to the truth of our infinite abundance it is imperative to then fan the flame of re-member-ance with as many of our brothers and sisters as possible. Mahareshi predicted it would only take one percent of the population expanding their consciousness by incorporating mindfulness to greatly impact the rest of the population. Author Malcolm Gladwell also suggested in his book *The Tipping Point* that when an unshakeable belief is held by ten percent of the population, this would be the critical mass necessary to shift the collective.[14] Researchers at Rensselaer Polytechnic Institute tested Gladwell's theory and concluded that "once that number grows above ten percent, the idea spreads like flame."[18] I believe spreading the light that emits from the alchemical wisdom contained in this book is the fastest way to save our planet and dramatically improve life for allLOVEus. Which is why I have chosen to empower others to freely gift this book, and why I hope I have also inspired and galvanized you to share this book with as many other you's and me's as possible by giving them your personal free book download code you already received (or can get) at goldenkey.gift! And don't forget, if you play the game with the *you*niverse and share your personal free book download code with someone that also opts to play the game, I am delighted to share 50% of the abundance generated with you from their monetary contribution, as explained in detail at goldenkey.gift.

HERE WE GROW

Congratulations exponentially multiplied! You have officially begun the next exciting chapter in your life journey where you have consciously chosen to alchemize your perspectives to unlock unlimited abundance — life will never be the same! In this exciting new chapter in your epic life saga it is imperative that you consistently remember to use your keys along the way to See the Oneness, Know the Illusion, Focus Your Flow, Align Your Intentions, Be, Be, Be, Trust the Mystery, and Love What Comes. As you start consciously tapping into abundance in all aspects of your daily life as a result of doing so, and in-joying all the ONEderFULL things you start attracting, also remember that the challenges are a necessary part of that equation too. It's vital that you remember that your challenges truly are blessings. Much like the practice of Kintsugi, or "Golden Joinery," which is the Japanese art of repairing broken pottery with gold, ultimately making the vessel even more beautiful than it was originally, you are also poised to shimmer brighter because of your golden challenges and life experiences when you implement these key perspectives. As you continue on your stellar life journey, be sure to re-member that everywhere you go, you're there waiting for yourself. Remember that fear is safe, and where attention goes energy flows. Remember that the best way you can help others is by demonstrating your butterflyness so that they can see what they too are destined to metamorphosize into. As Abraham-Hicks said, "You cannot suffer those suffering into wellness. You can't get sick enough to help the sick become well, and you can't get poor enough to help the poor become prosperous. And you can't feel bad enough to help the bad feel good. You've got to get on the other end of that. You've got to be a vibrational vessel through which that energy that uplifts flows. And when it flows, those who want it will gravitate to you. And then you'll be at the right place at the right time." [21] Your only real job is to manage your vibration. This is how mastery is unlocked. This is how you blossom into the inSPIRI-Tional heARTist from which abundance eternally overflows and that you are destined to become. Now that you have discovered who you truly are, the game really begins. You are the star. You are *it*. You are *everything*. Knowing this is your Golden Key to Master the *You*niverse.

THE FIRST KEY: *SEE THE ONENESS*

THE SECOND KEY: *KNOW THE ILLUSION*

THE THIRD KEY: *FOCUS YOUR FLOW*

THE FOURTH KEY: *ALIGN YOUR INTENTIONS*

THE FIFTH KEY: *BE, BE, BE*

THE SIXTH KEY: *TRUST THE MYSTERY*

THE SEVENTH KEY: *LOVE WHAT COMES*

THE GOLDEN KEY: *MASTER THE YOUNIVERSE*

Visit <u>goldenkey.gift</u> to:

❖ Get your personal free book download code to share with others

❖ Play the abundance manifestation game

❖ Share your success and see the inspiring results of others

❖ Get your physical Golden Key necklace

Want to Dive Even Deeper Down the Rabbit Hole?

1. Alexander, Eben. "81: Interview with best-selling author Dr. Eben Alexander discussing his miraculous near-death experience." Produced by Brandon Beachum. *The Positive Head Podcast.* January 6, 2016. Podcast, MP3 audio. http://positivehead. com/spread-the-positivity/2016/01/06/81-dr-eben-alexander

2. Alexander, Eben. *Proof of Heaven: A Neurosurgeon's Journey into the Afterlife.* New York, NY: Simon & Schuster Paperbacks, 2012.

3. Anka, Darryl (Bashar). "Bashar Communications." Last Updated December 5, 2020. http://vimeo.com/basharcommunications

4. Bostrom, Nick. "Are You Living in a Computer Simulation?" *Philosophical Quarterly* 53, no. 211, (2003): 243-255. http://www.simulation-argument.com/simulation.pdf

5. Braden, Gregg, host. *Missing Links.* 2017: Gaia, TV Series.

6. Borowski, Susan. "Quantum mechanics and the consciousness connection." Last modified July 16, 2012. http://www.aaas. org/quantum-mechanics-and-consciousness-connection

7. "Bully A Plant: Say No To Bullying." April 30, 2018: IKEA UAE, Video. http://www.youtube.com/ watch?v=Yx6UgfQreYY&feature=emb_title

8. Castaneda, Carlos. *The Power of Silence: Further Lessons of don Juan.* New York, NY: Washington Square Press, 1987.

9. Dass, Ram. *Be Here Now.* New York, NY: The Crown Publishing Group, 1971.

10. deGrasse Tyson, Neil. "The Most Astounding Fact - Neil deGrasse Tyson." Max Schlickenmeyer. March 2, 2012. http://www.youtube.com/watch?v=9D05ej8u-gU

11. Del Mar, Lewis. "Lewis Del Mar - Painting (Masterpiece) (Video)." Lewis Del Mar. October 20, 2016. Video. http://www.youtube.com/watch?v=NMvzY05i-q8

12. Dyer, Wayne. *The Power of Intention.* Hay House Inc., 2005.

13. Fox, Emmet. *The Golden Key.* Camarillo, CA: DeVorss Publications, 1931.

14. Gladwell, Malcolm. *The Tipping Point: How Little Things Can Make a Big Difference.* NY: Little, Brown and Company, 2000.

15. Goldner, Fred. "Pronoia." *Social Problems* 30, no. 1 (1982): 82–91. http://doi.org/10.2307/800186

16. Graham, Martha. "Martha Graham Reflects on Her Art and a Life in Dance." Last modified March 31, 1985. http://archive.nytimes.com/www.nytimes.com/library/arts/033185graham.html

17. Grant, Robert (@robertedwardgrant). "Randomness is simply the inability to perceive pattern." Instagram, November 12, 2019. http://www.robertedwardgrant.com/media

18. Groth, Aimee. "Scientists Reveal The 'Tipping Point' For Ideas Is When There's A 10% Consensus." *Business Insider.* (2011). http://www.businessinsider.com/scientists-reveal-the-tipping-point-for-ideas-is-when-theres-a-10-consensus-2011-7

19. Haramein, Nassim. "The Connected Universe | Nassim Haramein | TEDxUCSD." TEDx Talks. June 24, 2016. Video, http://www.youtube.com/watch?v=xJsl_klqVh0&list=PLLdX_IS7TQg-hguyNd4JUi8lXse-uVsUV

20. Hatchard, Guy et al. "The Maharishi Effect: A Model for Social Improvement. Time Series Analysis of a Phase Transition to Reduced Crime in Merseyside Metropolitan Area." *Psychology, Crime & Law 2,* no. 3 (1996): 165–74. http://doi.org/10.1080/10683169608409775.

21. Hicks, Esther (Abraham-Hicks). "Video Clips." Accessed on December 11, 2020. http://www.abraham-hicks.com/video

22. Jung, Carl. *Synchronicity: An Acausal Connecting Principle.* Princeton, NJ: Princeton University Press, 1960.

23. Lipton, Bruce. *The Biology of Belief: Unleashing the Power of Consciousness, Matter & Miracles.* Carlsbad, CA: Hay House, Inc., 2005. http://www.brucelipton.com/sites/default/files/biology_of_belief_cover_1st_chap.pdf

24. Lipton, Bruce. "161: Interview with best-selling author of The Biology of Belief, Dr. Bruce Lipton." Produced by Brandon Beachum. *The Positive Head Podcast.* April 27, 2016. Podcast, MP3 audio, 1:05:23. http://positivehead.com/spread-the-positivity/2016/04/27/161-dr-bruce-lipton

25. McKenna, Terence. "Terence McKenna - Unfolding The Stone." AronG. December 23, 2014. Video. http://www.youtube.com/watch?v=RdJWF0xDjcI

26. Rudd, Richard. *The Gene Keys: Embracing Your Higher Purpose.* London: Watkins Publishing Limited, 2013.

27. Rumi, Jalal al-Din. *The Essential Rumi, New Expanded Edition.* New York, NY: HarperCollins Publishers, 1995.

28. Rydall, Derek. *Emergence: Seven Steps for Radical Life Change.* New York, NY: Atria Books/Beyond Words, 2015.

29. Sagan, Carl. *The Demon-Haunted World: Science as a Candle in the Dark.* NY: The Random House Publishing Group, 1996.

30. Schucman, Helen. *A Course in Miracles: Based on the original handwritten notes of Helen Schucman.* West Sedona, AZ: The Circle of Atonement, Inc., 2017.

31. Singer, Michael. *The Surrender Experiment: My Journey into Life's Perfection.* NY: Shanti Publications, Inc., 2015.

32. Singer, Michael. *The Untethered Soul: The Journey Beyond Yourself.* Oakland, CA: New Harbinger Publications, Inc., 2007.

33. Stuver, Amber. "Einstein's twin paradox explained - Amber Stuver." TED-Ed. September 26, 2019. Video. http://www.youtube.com/watch?v=h8GqaAp3cGs

34. Supaman. "Dance like everybody is watching." Facebook, July 22, 2016, http://www.facebook.com/watch/?v=10155131608833636

35. Tanzi, Rudolph and Deepak Chopra. "You Can Transform Your Own Biology," last modified April 29, 2014. http://chopra.com/articles/you-can-transform-your-own-biology

36. Tolle, Eckhart. *The Power of Now: A Guide to Spiritual Enlightenment.* Vancouver, D.C., Canada: Namaste Publishing, 1999.

37. Tzu, Lao. *Tao Te Ching.* Translated by William Scott Wilson. Shambhala Publications, 2013.

38. Walsch, Neale Donald. *Conversations with God: An Uncommon Dialogue, Book 1.* New York, NY: G. P. Putman's Sons, 1996.

39. Walsch, Neale Donald. *The Little Soul and the Sun: A Children's Parable.* Charlottesville, VA: Hampton Roads Publishing Company, Inc., 1998.

40. Wartolowska, K. et al. "Use of Placebo Controls in the Evaluation of Surgery: Systematic Review." BMJ 348 (2014): 1-15. http://doi.org/10.1136/bmj.g3253

41. "Washington crime study shows 23.3% drop in violent crime trend due to meditating group." World Peace Group. Accessed December 9, 2020. http://www.worldpeacegroup.org/washington_crime_study.html

42. Watts, Alan. "Alan Watts Audio Recording." Accessed December 8, 2020. http://www.alanwatts.org/audio

43. Weir, Andy. "The Egg." Last modified August 15, 2009. http://www.galactanet.com/oneoff/theegg_mod.html